Vietnam Veteran Memoirs

-A Book of Miracles-

To Kay

MacClay

Mack Payne at Phu Bai

Vietnam Veteran Memoirs

-A Book of Miracles-

The Adventures of a Florida Flatlander

In Vietnam

By Mack W. Payne

ISBN-13: 978-1482581959

ISBN-10: 1482581957

Dedication

This book is dedicated to the memory of all those who fell in the Vietnam War, with a special salute to the following:

Captain Phil Bergfield

First Lt. Terry Martell

First Lt. Gary Tomlinson

CW2 Scott Schettig

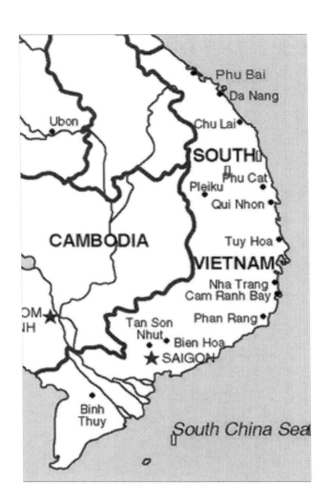

Contents

Preface

Before I get into describing the hot and heavy action I saw and participated in during my two-year adventure in Vietnam, I must give you a little background on how a Florida flatlander ended up in Vietnam.

I was born in Leesburg, Florida. I would have been born in Bushnell, Florida but there were no doctors in Bushnell at the time, and I doubt that they have any doctors in Bushnell today.

Before I was one year old my parents moved the family to Ocala, Florida where I was raised. As I grew up in Ocala, I never wanted to leave that fair little town. But now looking back over the years, I am strangely thankful for Marx and Engels because they kicked off a chain of events that took me away from my beloved hometown. And that's why I am so thankful, because after comparing my early life to the life I live now, I am so much happier today because I did not remain in Ocala.

Here is how a chain of events picked up young Mack Payne, just a regular, good old country boy from Ocala, Florida and thrust him into the middle of world affairs.

You may or may not be aware Marx and Engels were the two misguided fellows who came up with the flawed theory of Communism. Without them, there would not have been the narcotic theory of Communism tempting the masses with offers of such things as free medical care, free food, money for nothing, and other tempting freebies.

Without Communism, there would have been no Soviet Union. Without the Soviet Union, there would not have been a Cold War. Without a Cold War, there would not have been a necessity for the United States to maintain a large, standing military force.

And if the United States had not had to maintain a large, standing military force, it would not have been necessary for young Mack Payne from Ocala, Florida to be sucked up into the maelstrom of the Cold War and shown the world.

So that is why I did not fulfill my boyhood dream of spending my life in Ocala.

Today we hear a lot of talk about honoring the veterans and thanking them for the great service they did for their country. I am all for honoring the veterans because I am one but, sometimes I wonder.

The whole time I was in the service I received a paycheck each month, and it never bounced. Every time I had to move, the Army would take care of all the details and move me with few problems. Every time I got sick or hurt, they would provide topnotch medical care at no cost.

It was all very nice but had I not decided to go into the military voluntarily and serve my country, they would've thrown me in jail. Even though I was more than willing to serve, I always thought that if I didn't go forward and do my part, I would be in jail and that puts a different light on being a veteran to me.

The route I chose through which to serve my obligations to the country was through the ROTC program at the University of Florida. I graduated in 1966 and had the gold bars of a second lieutenant pinned on my shoulders. The next day I proceeded to Fort Benning, Georgia for the Infantry Officer's Basic Course.

Upon completion of the basic officer's course, I attended the three week intensive training offered by the US Army Jump School and graduated safely. With those silver wings pinned on my chest making me one of America's best, I proceeded up to Fort Bragg, North Carolina and joined up with A Company, 3rd Battalion, 325th Infantry of the famous 82nd Airborne Division.

Within a year, I had worn out my welcome at the 82nd Airborne Division and was invited to go some place else (it seems I had a little problem with orders: I only followed the ones I agreed with). Actually, my assignment was completed and my services were needed in Vietnam.

Naturally, I felt a little trepidation at the thought of going to Vietnam, but I went anyway, along with hundreds of thousands of other young men who also shared the same concerns of shortened lives.

Unfortunately, my willingness to serve was not shared by all. At the time, many people demonstrated against the war and burned their draft cards. Many became draft dodgers and ran off to Canada or other places, claiming it was against their conscience to participate in the Vietnam War.

I questioned the veracity of those claims. It was and still is my belief all those people who ran off to Canada had a big yellow stripe running down their backs and were just afraid to go. They were too worried about getting their lacy underwear mussed. As a whole I view them as nothing more than piles of chicken manure.

Okay, enough social commentary for the time being. If my views offend anyone, I offer my apologies (actually I don't but it sounds good to those with opposing view points).

I served two years in Vietnam. The first year was with the 4th Infantry Division from October 67 through

October of 68. My second year was with the 101st Airborne Division, from June of 1970 June of 1971.

After completing a will and other administrative requirements, I departed the USA from Fort Lewis, Washington. On my second tour I left from an Air Force base near Oakland, California.

When I left the Fort Lewis, Washington area for my first tour, I discovered it is possible for it to rain and not rain at the same time, for days at a time. That was a very interesting discovery for a Florida flatlander whose only previous travel consisted of a few trips to the south end of the Appalachian Mountains.

As we lifted off in that contract commercial airliner, it was full of young men with very serious looks on their faces, thinking about what might be facing them over in that land far, far away. In just a few short hours, we would be exploring a whole new and exotic world full of dangers, surprises and exciting adventures.

You would think the most direct route from Seattle-Tacoma to Vietnam would be a straight shot across the Pacific, crossing Hawaii, Wake Island, and places like that. But if you look at a globe you will see the best route is up north, so we took off from Seattle-Tacoma with a stopover in Anchorage, Alaska.

Then we proceeded on to Osaka, Japan. As we flew over Japan that night, you could look out and realize lots of people lived on that small island. We only stayed there for a few hours, and then proceeded on our way to our final destination, the massive airbase at Cam Ranh Bay. After many hours of flying we landed, all having sober thoughts on our minds and wondering if we were going to be attacked on the runway by Viet Cong.

Introduction

The writing of this book came as rather a surprise to me since I had never contemplated writing down my Vietnam memoirs. A happenstance event triggered my decision to record the memories of my three year roller coaster ride through history. It covers the two years I spent in Vietnam and the one in between.

I was living in Lake Placid, Florida and was a new member of a Toastmasters club over in Sarasota. I had been assigned to give a speech and since it is my first speech to the Sarasota club, I wanted to make sure it was a humdinger of a performance.

Even though I was a veteran of two tours in Vietnam and a Toastmaster for many years, I realized I had never spoken on the subject of my Vietnam experiences. It was not because I had a problem with it; it was that I assumed apparently few others cared to talk about it. I believe there is an "urban myth" floating around through the American psyche that all Vietnam veterans are screwed up in the head, and consequently, many are uncomfortable talking about the war with a veteran.

That was not the case with me. I never had any psychological problems resulting from my Vietnam service. I don't talk about it much because most everyone seems inclined to avoid the subject.

I decided to talk about one of my Vietnam adventures in the speech at Sarasota. In all my years of Toastmaster membership, dating back to the mid-80s, I had given over 100 speeches and never once had I talked about Vietnam.

I thought, what the hell, and decided to speak about one of my many interesting Vietnam adventures. I went back into the hard drive memory in my head and several different events came forth. I selected an incident I thought might make an interesting speech topic.

At first I wrote the speech to be whimsical in nature and make light of the event. But as I worked on it I realized it might have some inspirational value, so I changed the speech to emphasize the inspiring quality of the incident.

After my many years of study and practice I had already gotten over my stark fear of public speaking. I had come to enjoy it as much as a kid swinging on a rope over a river and dropping in. I wanted to use that same enthusiasm to deliver a memorable talk.

When I gave the speech I employed all the techniques used to bring the audience up, down, and back up again. It was well received by the audience.

That club was an advanced Toastmasters club with many accomplished individuals on the roster. After the speech I was approached by one of the members who identified herself as a publisher, and she advised me to expand on the speech subject because she thought it had merit. Suddenly a light of inspiration flashed.

I realized that though the Vietnam War has faded in our memories, it still has a good bit of historical relevance. I further deduced it has been off the front burner of American attention long enough that maybe some readers would be interested in learning about it from someone who had experienced the historical event in person.

I began to think about all the memorable things that happened to me in those three years, and based on what this publisher said to me, I decided to follow the example of Ulysses S. Grant and write my memoirs before I die.

That one comment from the club member infused me with a passion to record my memories of an exciting and turbulent time in America's history, and my own life.

What I intend to do is describe my experiences, thoughts, feelings and ideas so the reader can get an unvarnished look at one of the most trying times in our history from a different perspective.

The following commentary comes from a regular person thrown into a historical maelstrom, a regular guy, who went over, did his job, looked around, observed, and came home with mind and body intact. I hope you enjoy reading about my experiences, thoughts and observations of that time as much as I enjoyed living them.

1 - Good Morning Viet Nam

Our brand spanking new contracted Boeing 707 landed early in the morning at the massive Cam Ranh Bay Air Force Base in the province of Khanh Hoa on a clear morning in October of 1967.

We all sat there in our seats wondering when the first rounds were going to come in and blow up the airplane as it sat on the tarmac. After a seeming eternity of sitting and waiting, we were finally allowed to deplane.

As we left the airplane, we discovered we were in a tropical paradise with beautiful, blue skies, pure white sand, and palm trees blowing in the gentle breeze. The only indication of any (what were to us) foreigners was the few small, tan-skinned little people working at menial jobs around the area.

We were processed in and assigned quarters in temporary facilities while awaiting further assignment to our units in the field. It was a little disturbing to be there in our bright, clean, new uniforms with that fresh scrubbed look of newbies, and having to watch the veterans who had finished their year and were heading home.

They were tanned looking and walked around with smiles on their faces, not saying anything. It was a little discouraging to us because we knew we had a full year in front of us.

We experienced the familiar military tradition of hurry up and wait. We had to hurry up and get there, and then we just sat around our quarters waiting. It took a few days to get everybody assigned and shipped out to their units.

I was assigned to 4th Infantry Division headquartered up country in the Central Highlands, near the city of Pleiku. They sent this Florida Flatlander way up into the mountains. Despite all the stories I had heard warning about the hot and swampy conditions of Vietnam, after arriving at Pleiku in October, I realized there was a good reason we were issued cold-weather equipment. As they say in southeastern Alabama, it could get a "mite chilly" up there in the central highlands.

2 - The Fourth Infantry Division

The headquarters for the Fourth Infantry Division was located a few miles south of Pleiku, a fairly large town which is inland about 80 miles due west of the city of Qui Nhon along Highway 19. It was called Camp Mark N. Enari after a young officer killed in action during the Paul Revere campaign.

The area selected for the location of Camp Enari was on an open plain much like the terrain in Kansas. In its natural state, it was covered with a heavy layer of plains grass similar to what you might have found in Kansas before the homesteaders plowed up the State.

With military precision, the camp was laid out in a perfect 2 mile square. With typical military logic, the geniuses went in and scraped off all the native grass. I guess no one took into consideration there were two distinct seasons in the area: one very hot and dry, and the other very wet.

Everything went well until the onset of the first rainy season, and then the entire camp became one big mud bog. About the only way you could move around was to be pulled by a tracked vehicle. So they went on a crash program to pave streets, but they only paved one lane at a time. This caused many fights to break out among drivers who would refuse to yield their spot on the paved surface, because once they went off the paving, they would become stuck in the deep mud. It became a terrible mess that developed into a crisis situation for the generals.

But then thankfully, the rainy season subsided and the dry season came along. Suddenly, all that mud everybody hated turned into dust. Now this was not your regular household dust. It was fine and powdery and literally got into everything, including your food, clothes, ears, nose, and vehicle engines, to name a few.

So in their infinite wisdom, the division leadership went on a crash grass-planting program. They were so serious about it, that walking on the grass became a court-martial offense. This was the environment I was thrust into in October of 1967.

The camp had just survived another rainy season, and though everyone was happy the mud was gone, they had just been hit with the scourge of the dust. That was my introduction to Camp Enari. There were some other surprising events I was about to be introduced to.

Upon arrival at the 4th Infantry Division, I, along with all the other new guys, had to go through one week of orientation training.

That's where we were taught the things we needed to know about local conditions there in country. I had already received extensive training prior to my deployment, but this was designed to get us started on the right foot with the Division in the Central Highlands. The most memorable thing about the training was that it was canceled halfway through because of a little difficulty that had arisen at a place called Dak To.

It seems a major battle had broken out and they needed all hands on deck immediately. I guess I was living right because instead of being sent straight to the killing fields of Dak To, I was assigned to the 4th S&T Battalion.

The S&T stands for Supply and Transport, which was not my first choice of Army duty. At the University of Florida I had majored in Business Administration and had excelled sufficiently in the ROTC to be offered a regular army commission. With that type of commission, the Army takes a much closer look at your background when making branch assignments. For that reason, I had been offered a Regular Army Commission in the Quartermaster Corps.

At the time I didn't know much about the Quartermaster Corps and had always hoped to serve in the Infantry Branch. At first, I refused the offer. Fortunately for me, a wise old sergeant-major in the ROTC Office at the UF advised me to accept the offer because regular commissions were hard to come by, plus

I would be allowed to serve two years in the combat arm of my choice.

I accepted the offer and served my Infantry service with the 82nd Airborne Division at Fort Bragg and then headed overseas. Just prior to my deployment to Vietnam I had pinned on the Quartermaster Corps insignia.

Upon arrival at the 4th S&T Battalion, I discovered the battalion commander to be someone with whom I had a shared history. Unfortunately that history compels me to allow him to remain nameless, except for the sobriquet Colonel Pond Scum. It was my opinion that was an appropriate name for him.

During my tenure as a second lieutenant with the 82nd Airborne Division at Fort Bragg, North Carolina, I did not excel in receiving stellar officer efficiency reports. When my turn came to go to Vietnam, Colonel Pond Scum was working at the U.S. Army Personnel Department at the Pentagon. He supervised my transition to my permanent Regular Army branch assignment in the Quartermaster Corps.

One day at Fort Bragg I received a phone call from the personnel department at the Pentagon. An individual said I was being transferred to my basic branch, the Quartermaster Corps, and was immediately being reassigned to a petroleum distribution unit located at Qui Nhon, Vietnam.

The officer making the phone call introduced himself and I immediately forgot his name as I was wont to do. Lo and behold, when I arrived for duty at the 4th S&T Battalion I made an interesting discovery. While being interviewed by the Battalion Commander, he informed me he was the very officer who called me from the Pentagon that day and supervised my transfer from the Infantry Branch to my permanent branch, the Quartermaster Corps. He also assigned me to the petroleum distribution unit at Qui Nhon and through some quirk of fate in the assignment process, I had been reassigned to the 4th S&T Battalion at Pleiku where he was the commander.

I got the distinct impression he was not overjoyed to have me as a member of his command because he was aware of my unspectacular record up to that time.

I soon discovered him to be a despicable human being. He had apparently taken it upon himself as a personal crusade to insure that all officers in the Army maintained his perceived high standards of behavior and performance.

An incident involving a lieutenant in the Battalion demonstrated the commander's devotion to his crusade. The lieutenant worked at the Post Exchange, or store, to civilians. Unfortunately, he had become involved in some nefarious activities and was facing judgment.

The young lieutenant was being sent back to the States and as a courtesy he was invited to the Battalion's monthly party to greet new arrivals and say goodbye to departing members.

Even though he was disgraced by the accusations against him, he did show up at the party to say goodbye to his friends before he returned to the States. The Battalion Commander, who was also at the party, displayed his vicious cruelty. In front of everyone there he openly ridiculed and laughed at the young officer for his shortcomings. He called him names and humiliated him to the point of almost driving the young man to tears. I was appalled.

It was a very uncomfortable situation for everyone in attendance and it demonstrated what a lowlife individual the Battalion Commander was proving to be. I felt his behavior was totally out of order and uncalled for in the situation.

Later, I too would run afoul of this vile excuse for a leader. He would discover to his misfortune you'd better be very careful if you choose to mess with Mack Payne, Florida Flatlander.

This worthless piece of human debris in the form of the Battalion Commander had the unusual practice of requiring visitors to his office to sit in a chair placed on his flank side, to the rear of his line of sight. He would face forward at his desk and speak to the visitor and never face the person. He was a strange dude.

That was my welcome to the 4th S&T Battalion. My initial assignment was to the division petroleum point (that assignment would not last long). We were in charge of ensuring the division's vehicles had adequate fuel, oil and lubricating materials.

Our petroleum point was located at the main entrance to Camp Enari. It was there that early on, I was introduced to the "Vietnam Attitude" by a bazaar incident. In the wartime environment of the time, each unit would run their own telephone lines around the post. The engineers provided poles for individual units to run their land lines wherever they were needed. Soon there were hundreds of telephone lines attached to the poles.

At the main gate near our petroleum point, there were two telephone poles on either side of the gate, supporting a large number of these telephone lines. The telephone wires created a combined cable about 6 inches in diameter.

On my second or third day at the petroleum point, a large truck carrying a wrecked helicopter on a low-boy trailer was leaving the camp. The rotor blades had been torn off the wrecked helicopter, leaving only the rotor mast sticking up as the driver approached the gate. He knew the low hanging cable might get snagged on the helicopter's rotor column.

As I watched this incident unfold, the driver very carefully drove to a point where the rotor mast was close to the wires. He stopped the truck and discovered the rotor head protruded slightly higher than the massive, combined cable of telephone wires. He could not drive through the gate and clear the cable.

The driver surveyed the situation, paced a little and thought it over. I was going over to offer our assistance but before I could do that, he climbed back in the truck, revved his engine, and to my amazement charged forward through the gate.

The rotor mast did snag the telephone lines and in the process the cable was broken, along with several poles in both directions. I was stunned as I watched the disaster happen, and was further amazed at the lack of alarm everyone in the area displayed. The truck driver proceeded on as if nothing had happened.

It was my initiation to a common "Vietnam attitude." I began to notice almost every time I would bring up the fact that something was being done improperly I would get the response, "Don't worry about it, this is Vietnam."

It was ironic that we had received extensive training for Vietnam back in the States, only to discover the common attitude, we don't do that here, this is Vietnam, prevailing in the very arena for which we had trained.

3 - My First Month at Camp Enari

The mission of the 4th S&T Battalion was to provide the division with logistical support. That included such things as supplies, food, petroleum, transportation services, and graves registration, to name a few. Except for the psychotic battalion commander, most of the officers in the unit were outstanding individuals (except for a few suck ups to the commander).

There was one officer who was a little unique but he became one of my good friends in the 4th S&T Battalion. His name was Lt. James Nakada. He was a short-statured American of Japanese descent from California. He walked around like a sad sack in a permanent state of depression. He reminded me of the cartoon character who had a perpetual rain cloud over his head. He was very low keyed and had a subtle sense of humor which I liked.

Lt. Nakada and I had many interesting and exciting adventures, some of which will be described in later chapters.

Another interesting aspect of life at Camp Enari was base security. All the front-line combat units of the division were deployed in various local areas, doing their thing in places like the aforementioned Dak To, and the Ia Drang Valley. That meant the units assigned to the base camp were responsible for the security of their portion of the camp's security area.

There were five major commands at the base camp, including the headquarters of the three infantry brigades and division artillery, plus the division support command. A circle with a 10 mile radius was drawn around the base and divided into five pieces like a big pie. Each major command was assigned its piece of the pie and required to insure their areas were safe and not harboring any of the bad guys with those pesky 122 mm rockets and such.

The 4th S&T Battalion was a part of the Division Support Command, so that was the piece of the pie we were responsible for helping to secure. And therein was my first big Vietnam adventure.

It was the practice of the Division Support Command to send out recon patrols consisting of one officer and one dozen soldiers. The mission of the recon patrols was to walk out through the woods and insure there were no bad guys present.

It was a battalion policy that every new officer accompany an experienced officer on a recon patrol out in the woods to become oriented to the area, and learn the procedures. Shortly after I arrived I was invited to participate in one of these patrols, along with another unnamed Lt.

Earlier I mentioned my situation of being a Regular Army Officer in the Quartermaster Corps and having been detailed to the Infantry Branch for a seasoning as a career Army officer.

I completed my infantry detail with the 82nd Airborne Division. Next to the 101st Airborne Division, the 82nd is one of the most storied units in the US Army and they went out of their way to ensure everyone assigned to that unit maintained that stellar reputation.

At the Infantry Officers Basic Course, I was trained in infantry tactics with a specialty in Vietnam conditions, before joining the 82nd Airborne Division. We had been told the Infantry School Leadership had been castigated by Gen. Westmoreland, commander of forces in Vietnam. Apparently the General was not happy with the performance of the products of their school in the fields of Vietnam.

The school leadership increased the intensity of the training with an orientation toward Vietnam style warfare. I was well-versed in the correct procedures of conducting combat operations in such a location as Vietnam.

After the training at Fort Benning most of my time spent with the 82nd Airborne Division was focused toward intensive training for eventual deployment to Vietnam. I considered myself to be a trained and qualified infantry officer.

The big day at Camp Enari came for my orientation as a recon patrol leader. It involved a recon operation that would take us on a route of about eight miles into the countryside. As preparations were being made for the mission, the officer leading the patrol provided me with a sketchy orientation briefing. Since this was my first encounter with the real thing, I had a few questions for him.

I began to ask questions about different tactical considerations like flank security and so forth. I soon began to realize Quartermaster Officers did not seem to be familiar with those basic tactical procedures. I was slightly alarmed because we were going out into a situation where if you didn't know the correct procedures, it might turn deadly.

The more questions I asked, the more disturbed the officer became. Finally I was asked to cease asking questions and just go along and watch "how we do it" in Viet Nam. Being a nice guy, I stopped asking questions and hopped in the truck and headed out to the drop-off point with this group of real killers from the supply yard and petroleum point.

Later I discovered that the patrol leader had received a direct commission to the Quartermaster Corps. One day he was a civilian and the next he was supervising the delivery of military supplies. It was no wonder he did not seem to know what I was talking about with my questions about infantry tactics

In the beginning I walked along with the patrol leader at the front of the column. We were walking down a path, which I instantly recognized as the number one violation of Jungle Fighting 101.

The officer was not pleased with my suggestion that we get off the path. He apparently liked walking on the path. It was at that point he suggested I go to the rear of the column and escort the individual carrying the spare radio just in case he got lost on the path.

Not wanting to be disruptive, I did as I was told and went back to the rear of the column and accompanied a large heavy set young soldier carrying the extra radio.

As the patrol moved along the path, I kept thinking to myself, is this really how they do it here? Isn't this a little wrong to be walking down this path? It was counter to everything I had been taught. All of a sudden a hail of gunfire came in our direction.

We all hit the ground, except for the oversized young man with the spare radio. He had moved ahead of me on the path just before the gunfire. As soon as the bullets began to fly through the trees above with their distinctive whizzing sounds, he decided he was going to leave the area. He turned around and began running as fast as he could in my direction. He looked like a raging rhino headed my way at full speed.

I got up to stop him and he crashed into me like Ray Lewis tackling a quarterback and knocked me flat on my back. I realized we might need that radio, so as he was running over me I reached up with both arms and grabbed his legs, causing him to fall forward. I was able to convince him to stay where he was because it was safer, and we might need the spare radio.

As we all lay there on the ground trying to be small targets, I listened for the first time to that unforgettable sound of bullets passing through the trees above. Being the new guy I was thinking, wasn't this a great opportunity to observe how they handle such situations here in Vietnam?

After a few moments of inactivity on our part I decided to move up to the front of the column to find out what was going on, and observe the seasoned pros in action. So as the bullets continued to sing through the trees above, I low-crawled along the path to where our fearless leader was conducting the operation.

I made my way to the patrol headquarters location and found the patrol leader and his NCO looking intently up into the trees. I quickly glanced in the trees thinking there might be something up there but saw nothing that might be a threat to our safety.

I inquired as to what he looking for in the trees. He replied, that's "what they advised" him to do. I asked him who "they" were and he stated they were the people in the operations center back in the base camp. I was a little perplexed as to how the people back in the operations center in the base camp would know there may be something in the trees above us. I reasoned that to locate the enemy, it might be more important to consider the direction from which the bullets were coming.

The lieutenant in charge was in no mood to discuss the subject. At that time I made a suggestion we might move forward and engage the bad guys. He looked at me and said, "go ahead." I said okay, and grabbed two enterprising young troops nearby and proceeded to initiate the infamous grenade incident.

Before I moved out to engage the enemy, I decided to shake them up a little bit first by chunking a hand grenade in their direction, with the intention of momentarily distracting the opposing force's attention.

After warning everyone to keep their heads down, I grabbed a hand grenade, pulled the pin, and with everything I had, threw it up the hill in the direction of the bad guys.

Unfortunately the hand grenade hit a tree, fell to the ground and began rolling down the path in our direction. I feared I was going to kill all of us on my first recon patrol with my own hand grenade.

But as usual, my guardian angel was watching over us all and it was discovered that in my haste to toss the hand grenade, I had failed to pull the pin all the way out. Such an act is not like in the movies where the heroes pull pins out of hand grenades with their teeth. Those pins are very securely placed in hand grenades and are very difficult to pull out. So we were spared by my inability to pull the pin completely out with a shaking and wet hand.

After a short moment to regain my composure, the two troopers and I proceeded up the hill. We walked carefully and slowly, expecting to be cut down at any moment by enemy fire. Apparently the opposing forces were not interested in further engagement.

overwhelmed with the thought of what a great person this Richard Petty must be. Here I was just another face in the crowd of his many fans, yet at the zenith of his popularity he took time to write me a personal letter.

Being a skeptic by nature I figured he probably sent that same letter in response to all his fan mail and just changed the greeting. But upon close inspection of the original document I began to think it might actually be the real thing due to the misspellings and typos. I also noticed the absense of initials at the lower left of the page as was the style of the time to identify the typist.

I then began to wonder, could it be the great man himself had actually written me a personal letter. It really doesn't matter who wrote the letter I am still one of his biggest fans.

I decided to include the actual letter in this book so the reader could see why I was so impressed with this man from North Carolina.

January 13, 1968

Dear Mack,

    I will run a 68 Roadrunner with the
426 cu. in. at Daytona. In the smaller races
I will run the 404 cu. in. engine.

    Ford will most likely run Mercury fronts
on there cars at Daytona. They will be using the
same engine.

    I feel that I will be able to run with the
Fords just as good this year as I did last year.
If I felt that I didntt have a chance I'd be
foolish to get out there.

    I will plan to run all the races this year
as I have always done. The more you run the more
you learn about your car. It also keeps my reflexea
in good working order.

    I will sure be trying to top my records of
last year. With hard work and lady luck we chould
be able to go just as good.

    You boys hold down the front over there. Your
doing a great job.

Yours truly,

#43

5 - The Third Brigade

Before I relate my adventures with the Third Brigade out on the coastline at Duc Pho, I must give you a little background as to how things developed that resulted in the Division's Third Brigade being orphaned out at there.

At that particular time there was a large American military presence in Vietnam. During the buildup of forces, units were rushed over and sometimes things did not work out as planned.

The major combat unit of the US Army at that time was the infantry division. They were normally composed of three infantry brigades: one brigade of artillery referred to as division artillery or "divarty" and a support brigade known as the division support command.

As the US military buildup began in earnest in 1965 and 1966, many divisions were sent over quickly, and sometimes all the elements of a division did not arrive at the same place in the country.

Such a situation occurred with the 4th and 25th Infantry Divisions. After the two divisions got to Vietnam, things settled down and it was discovered the 3rd brigades of both divisions were switched in transit. The missing brigade of the 4th Infantry Division was somewhere down south near the 25th Infantry Division, and the missing brigade of the 25th division was up North above Qui Nhon.

In their infinite wisdom the Army leadership in charge of the Divisions decided that rather than physically moving the lost brigades to their assigned units, it was easier to just switch designations and leave the affected brigades where they were. With the stroke of a pen, the 3rd Brigade of the 4th Infantry Division became the 3rd Brigade of the 25th Infantry Division down south. And vice versa, the 3rd brigade of the 25th Division morphed into the 3rd Brigade of the 4th Infantry Division. So now, all could get down to the business at hand of dealing with the bad guys.

Even with that re-designation of units, the 3rd Brigade of the 4th Infantry Division was still far away from the Division Headquarters. To get to division headquarters from the 3rd Brigade headquarters by Jeep, one would have to take Highway 1 south about 80 miles down to Qui Nhon, then hang a right on Highway 19 and go about 80 miles up in the Highlands to get to the 4th Division Headquarters.

So as the situation presented itself, the new 3rd Brigade of the 4th Division was administratively attached to the 4th Division, but they were too far away to be in the operational control area of the Division.

Thus the newly attached 3rd Brigade was farmed out to another command for combat operations, one of which was the Americal Division up near Chu Lai.

So that was the situation I found myself in when I was sent out to the 3rd Brigade of the 4th Infantry Division at Duc Pho. It was administratively attached to the 4th Infantry Division but operationally it was separate, meaning we very seldom had much contact with the 4th S&T Battalion back of the 4th Infantry Division at Pleiku.

When I first arrived at the 3rd brigade out by the coastline, it was manned by an outstanding group of soldiers formerly with the 25th Infantry Division. Many of those individuals never changed their 25th Division patches due to their strong allegiance to their old unit. I admired such strong feelings about a unit, so it did not bother me that they kept their old patches on their uniforms.

The length of a tour of duty in Vietnam was one year to the day. This resulted in people coming and going all the time, with replacements coming in to replace the departees on a regular basis.

I began to suspect that as the outstanding soldiers formally with the 25th Division rotated out, there was some hanky panky going on with their replacements. The previously mentioned commander of the 4th S&T

Battalion began sending out replacements for the departing 25th Division personnel. It soon became obvious the quality of the personnel being sent out to us was far below that of the ones who were leaving.

That presented some personnel challenges, but we overcame them. Sadly, in my opinion it demonstrated the lowlife quality of the 4th S&T Battalion commander. Rather than sending good people out to the Third Brigade, he would send rejects he did not want back at the base camp.

Since the Third Brigade was operating separately from the 4th Division, it was organized with a 30% slice of the support services found with the Division. This new organization was referred to as the Third Brigade Task Force.

An S&T company was formed to be a part of a provisional support battalion supporting the Third Brigade Task Force.

The mission of the S&T Company was to make sure the Brigade Task Force was supplied with food, clothing, petroleum and other type supplies.

It was very rewarding work for me because it was a smaller unit and we were closer to the people we were supporting. We could get a better feel for the work and we knew they appreciated what we were doing for them.

Another attractive feature of duty with the Third Brigade was the weather. It was wonderful down by the South China Sea with its constant cool breezes. Compared to the cool, rainy and miserable weather up in the Central Highlands, it was like being in a tropical paradise.

I always considered it a shame that a war was going on in this beautiful place. The white sandy beaches were so nice and the water was so clear, I believe there could have been a tremendous vacation industry there. Unfortunately some people believed the ends justified the means so they had to screw it up.

Another feature of Army life in smaller units was the food. I had always preferred company level mess halls, and that's what we had with the Third Brigade, and the food was outstanding.

We were fortunate to have a mess sergeant who had spent many years at the Natick Food Labs in Massachusetts. He was an expert in the art of producing delicious food so we always ate well and many times he would treat us with gastronomical delights.

Once he somehow managed to acquire a large quantity of king-sized lobster tails. He prepared them better than you would find in a fancy restaurant. I gorged myself with those treats from the ocean. Unfortunately, to this day I do not like lobster tails because I ate so many of them that day.

Life out at Duc Pho was good. Every night we had free first-run movies that you would normally pay big bucks for back in the States. It became an enjoyable ritual to set up a projector in front of the mess hall and enjoy those first-run movies outdoors while the cool breezes kept us comfortable. Each morning after evenings the movies were shown, the company area would be covered with Coke cans and beer bottles. No one complained about having to police the area after the morning formation.

Another nice feature of life at Duc Pho was sundry packs. Since we were in an area not served by post exchanges or stores, we were supplied with these cornucopias at no cost, containing all the things you would normally buy in a store. They included everything from writing paper to Beech Nut Chewing Tobacco. Their only drawback was an encouragement of theft. The locals would trade anything for a sundry pack.

We were located near the small village and it was very interesting because sometimes we would go there and acquire a good sample of the local culture.

I was fascinated with this exotic land and loved traveling around and seeing it close-up. The pay officer duty assignment was one of my favorites because it gave me a bonafide reason to travel around the countryside every month. Our company had personnel assigned all over the Central Highlands and Qui Nhon. Someone had to deliver their pay to them. At that time it was Army policy to pay monthly in cash and each company-sized unit would appoint a pay officer to pay each member of the unit.

I was familiar with the job because I had performed it many times back at Fort Bragg, where it was a ceremonious occasion and treated as a holiday known as "Payday Procedures."

On the first day of each month all the pay officers in the 82nd Airborne Division would assemble at the division finance office to receive the payroll. That was a serious responsibility because each pay officer would be assuming the responsibility for a large amount of cash.

There was no training for pay officer duty so in the beginning I just did what everyone else was doing. You signed a receipt and they handed you a big pile of money with a list showing the amount of payment for each individual.

First you would count the big stack of money and then break it down for each individual payment. It was a laborious and time-consuming task because the typical company had around 150 members. Pay officer duty was not a sought after endeavor. In most cases it was assigned to the most junior officer in a unit, but I liked handling all that money and seeing the happiness it brought the recipients.

I was assigned pay officer duty at Duc Pho and decided to do something out of the box. In all my time as a pay officer I never encountered an instance of miscounting by the Finance Office personnel. I decided the time saved by not recounting the money upon receipt was worth the risk. In a follow-on risk assessment, I saw no reason to break down the large pile of money into individual payment amounts. I decided to pay each person off the top of the money pile. This system worked quite well. I saved a great deal of time and aggravation and never ended up with an incorrect amount of money.

I also reasoned it was not necessary to announce to everyone in Central Vietnam I was a pay officer carrying tens of thousands of dollars on my person. All my fellow pay officers would carry out their duties armed with a side arm and accompanied by an armed guard.

I chose to carry out my duties incognito. The only item I took with me as I distributed the pay around the country was my old, beat up Samsonite brief case. I was not armed and I traveled alone with no guards. I never came up short, all were paid on time, and I saved lots of time and misery. That's how I did it in Vietnam, and I must say my system worked fine for me. A shrink once described me as a risk taker. I guess he knew what he was talking about.

Nothing lasts forever, including our halcyon days at Duc Pho. Not long after I arrived, the word came out we were moving north. That was fine with me because it moved us further away from the Division Headquarters and Col. Pond Scum at Pleiku.

One of the reasons we were moving north was that a new unit was coming into the area. The Americal Division was just arriving in Vietnam and the Third Brigade (Provisional) was moving north to make room for the new unit.

The new division would be headquartered at Chu Lai, which was located up the road from us about 20 or 30 miles.

We assisted the new unit as it moved into the area and got setup. I had the opportunity to meet a Capt. Medina and one of his lieutenants named William Calley.

Capt. Medina was a very serious-minded individual who was a company commander at the time. When I met him he was busy with getting his men moved in and set up. Lt. Calley appeared to be a forgettable, nondescript individual.

If you are familiar with the history of the Vietnam War you probably are aware of the massacre at My Lai. Little did I know that the Capt. Medina and Lt. Calley I met during the arrival of the Americal Division would be involved in one of the most hideous atrocities of the war.

Lt. Calley was a product of the lower standards the Army put in place when they expanded and needed more officers. Somehow William Calley made it through the system, to the detriment to all those dead citizens of My Lai - so much for lowered standards.

It was fascinating to me how normal-seeming people can get wrapped up in such situations. I was not that impressed with Lt. Calley, however Capt. Medina appeared to be a good officer trying to do his best.

As the time for the move got closer we began to feverishly prepare for the relocation to a new home at LZ Baldy. It was decided we were not going to move any of our loading and storage facilities so it was a matter of packing up our portable equipment and heading north.

It is very interesting how the Army changes nomenclature from time to time. In my first tour, combat bases were referred to as landing zones or LZs. In my second tour the very same installations were referred to as fire bases. I always got a kick out of the evolution of Army nomenclature.

Another one of those little things I found fascinating was the mail service. On my first tour Lyndon Johnson was president and it would take three days to receive a letter from home. Richard Nixon was president during my second tour and it would take five days to receive a letter. I always wondered if Presidents could really affect the mail service.

Our new home was going to be about 50 miles up the coast at an LZ with two names. It was known as Hill 63 and also the more descriptive name, LZ Baldy. We were displacing the 1st Calvary Division as it was moving South in preparation for the invasion of Cambodia.

The 1st Calvary Division was famous for being the first air mobile division. They could move their entire division with their own aircraft. For this reason they were the fire brigade of Vietnam who were always called upon to go first into the hot areas. They gained a well-deserved reputation as a highly successful fighting organization.

From my observations it was clear the personnel of the 1st Calvary Division also had a well-deserved reputation for craziness. The movie Apocalypse Now presented one of the most realistic portrayals of the type people in the 1st Cav.

If you are familiar with the movie you are aware of the scene where a mythical US Army cavalry squadron attacked a Vietcong position. The attack was led by a squadron commander by the name of Lieut. Col. Bill Kilgore, played by the great actor Robert Duvall. If you want to know about the 1st Cavalry Division in Vietnam, watch that scene of the movie. It was a very realistic portrayal of how the 1st Cavalry Division operated.

I mention the movie because that battle scene was the best of any Vietnam War movie I have seen. Many missed the mark trying to be political or dramatic but Robert Duvall hit the nail on the head in Apocalypse Now.

That was my first introduction to airmobile operations. Soon after arrival, my counterpart in the departing 1st Cavalry Division was giving me an orientation of the area. Suddenly in mid-sentence he jumped out of the Jeep and crawled under the vehicle. I wondered why and soon learned the reason when a large Cinook helicopter landed nearby. The prop wash began blowing small pebbles and rocks in our direction and they were like bullets flying through the air. After that I always took cover when a helicopter of any size landed nearby.

The 1st Cavalry Division moved out rapidly and left LZ Baldy to us. We spent approximately two months there and like my entire time in Vietnam, it was full of interesting events.

The further north we moved, the more combat activity the Third Brigade experienced. One indication was the appearance of more body bags at the medical station next to our supply yard. The bodies would be stacked like cord wood, awaiting shipment to Chu Lai. It was a little disturbing to see the refrigerated supply trucks go next door and load up with dead bodies, right after they delivered rations to us.

When I asked if it wasn't against regulations to put dead bodies in the same vehicles that transport food, I received the stock answer - "This is Vietnam and that's the way it's done here."

I always thought it was twisted logic when I would hear that comment. Before going to Vietnam we were trained in the proper methods of operating in Vietnam. Now I was in Vietnam and the attitude seemed to be, we don't do that here, this is Vietnam.

Living conditions at LZ Baldy were not nearly as nice as those at Duc Pho, but we we carried on with our jobs to the best of our abilities.

I'm going to take a detour out of my description of life in the Third Brigade Provisional at LZ Baldy and tell you about some things I saw and learned during the notorious Tet Offensive of 1968.

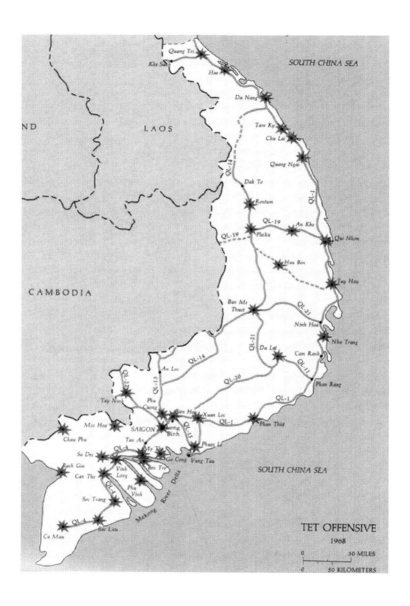

QL-14

Quang Tri
Khe Sanh
Hue

SOUTH CHINA SEA

LAOS

Da Nang

Tam Ky
Chu Lai

Quang Ngai

Dak To

Kontum

QL-1

QL-19
An Khe
Pleiku
Qui Nhon

QL-19

Hau Bon

Tuy Hoa

CAMBODIA

Ban Me
Thuot

QL-21

Ninh Hoa

QL-21
Da Lat
Cam Ranh
Nha Trang

QL-11

An Loc
QL-14
QL-20
Phan Rang

QL-13
Tay Ninh
Phu
Cuong
Bien Hoa
Xuan Loc
QL-1

QL-1
Phan Thiet

Moc Hoa
SAIGON
Tan An
Binh
QL-15
Phuoc Le

Chau Phu
My Tho
Go Cong
Vung Tau

QL-4
Sa Dec
Ben Tre
SOUTH CHINA SEA

Rach Gia
Vinh
Long
Can Tho
Phu
Vinh

QL-4
Soc Trang

QL-3
Ca Mau
Bac Lieu

Mekong River Delta

TET OFFENSIVE

1968

0   50 MILES

0   50 KILOMETERS

6- Tet of '68

Most any student of that time in our history is well aware of the Tet Offensive of '68. It was a remarkable event and I happened to be slap dab in the middle of the pathetic affair.

Tet is a special holiday for the Vietnamese when they celebrate their new year. It was a very festive occasion and up until 1968 both sides would declare an unofficial timeout from the fighting to celebrate the holiday.

But things were different in 1968. The northern forces were getting desperate because they found there was no way they could defeat the American war machine on the battlefields of Vietnam.

At the time, I drew a conclusion concerning the motivation of the northern forces to engage in such operations and those assumptions were later confirmed by writings of General Giap, the commander of northern forces.

I concluded it was a last gasp effort of the North to defeat the Americans and the South Vietnamese Army. For the first time, the northern forces came out of their rat holes and caves in the jungles and attacked most of the towns of any size throughout the country.

You have to give them credit; they conducted an extremely well-organized operation from top to bottom. And showing how devious they could be, it was executed during the country's most revered holiday.

General Giap later said if it had failed, they would have quit the war. From a military standpoint the operation was a total failure for the North. They held no ground and they were defeated at every point of attack with a total loss of over 50,000 soldiers.

According to his writings Gen. Giap was ready to throw in the towel after this tremendous defeat until he heard the comments of Walter Cronkite. You may remember that famous broadcast on the CBS Evening News when Mr. Cronkite announced in a very serious manner, "we have lost the war."

Suddenly Gen. Giap realized he did not lose, but rather the Americans had lost their nerve, and he decided to continue fighting. That was in 1968. The fighting continued until 1973 when the Paris Peace Accords were signed around that famous round table in Paris, France.

It is my belief that good old Walter Cronkite and his fellow defeatists have the blood on their hands of all the young men who were killed in Vietnam during that five-year period.

However, that's enough political talk, for now. I want to tell you about the exciting adventures I experienced during that historic event.

First, a little background: remember my friend Lt. Nakada? He had been assigned as our liaison officer at the big military supply depot at Qui Nhon, the large city about 100 miles South of LZ Baldy. I liked that because on occasion I would have to go to Qui Nhon on business and Lieutenant Nakada was always there with a Jeep and he could squire me around to take care of the business and see the town.

Qui Nhon was not the largest supply depot in Vietnam but it definitely stocked a huge amount of military equipment. The military had unbelievable quantities of supplies there. It was breathtaking to gaze at the large storage yards and survey the incredible amounts of US equipment on hand.

At the time of the Tet Offensive, we were located up at LZ Baldy and received limited news about what was going on in the rest of the country. Suddenly we began receiving reports of the hostile activity going on inside towns like Danang, Qui Nhon, Saigon, and many of other large cities.

At first we were a little amused about this because normally combat activity was restricted to the outback areas and in the mountains like where we were, at the isolated LZ Baldy location.

We were used to hearing the symphony of the battlefield at these forward bases so we got a little kick out of learning that our urban associates were receiving a little of the business end of the enemy.

There was little hostile activity occurring at LZ Baldy. One night a single errant mortar round came into our company area and landed on the front bumper of one of our trucks, causing considerable damage to that unlucky vehicle. That was the extent of the Tet Offensive at LZ Baldy.

At the time, we did not realize the seriousness of the situation. When it became necessary for me to make one my regular trips down to Qui Nhon, I never really gave the matter a second thought as I flew down to the Qui Nhon airport. Armed with my trusty Samsonite briefcase, the plan was to have Lt. Nakada meet me at the airport with his usual Jeep and we would go on our way.

Qui Nhon was a pretty good-sized city in addition to the large military presence located nearby. The Air Force ran a large operation there with an aerial port very much like a civilian airport terminal.

Nakada's office was conveniently located in an office building just a few blocks from the airport, but I always preferred to have him pick me up when I landed, so I could ride around in style. It was exciting to go to the big exotic city and see the Asian culture on display. It was always hustling and bustling with people, street vendors with their pushcarts, and taxis running around everywhere. It was an interesting change from the isolation of LZ Baldy.

When I arrived that day, at the beginning of Tet, I was like an innocent little lamb, not realizing I was about to enter a very strange twilight zone arena of combat. After landing at the airport, I got off the C-130 as usual and walked into the terminal. I was immediately struck by the fact the normal crowds were not there.

I was still not suspecting anything strange and no one said anything to indicate things were different, so I with my briefcase walked to the entrance looking for Lt. Nakada. He was nowhere to be seen.

I thought, no problem, his office is only a few blocks away, I'll just walk. As I'm leaving the terminal, there in front of me in the street was a barricade manned by combat troops and machine guns facing out toward the street.

Still not really grasping the gravity of the situation, I merely proceeded to walk across the barriers in front of the machine guns and on down the street, heading for the office building. No one had yet said anything to me about not going there or being careful and there was no indication of ongoing combat.

Approximately one block from the entrance of the airport, I would make a right-hand turn, go approximately two blocks, and then make a left-hand turn into the office complex where Nakada and his trusty Jeep would hopefully be waiting.

Normally those streets would be jammed packed with all sorts of human activity going on, but as I made the right turn at that first block I looked both ways and it was like the twilight zone - not a soul in sight either way.

Still not thinking things were really out of the ordinary, I continued along the next two blocks until I came to the street where I made the left turn into the office complex. There, to my surprise, I was faced with another imposing barricade, fully manned by more combat troops with enough firepower to fight a small war. Furthermore, they were all aimed at me, a clueless Lieutenant heading their way, armed with only my beat up briefcase.

Again, being totally clueless, I figured it must be a drill and was thinking, how efficient the commanders were here at the military depot to run one of these training drills just as I was coming into town.

I walked past the soldiers and their lineup of machine guns and concertina. Still no one challenged me, no one asked why I was there, and no one suggested that maybe I should get out of the way. I figured it must have been my imposing appearance that prevented me from being blown away by several machine guns.

But wait! It only gets better. Entering Nakada's office, I found him at his desk, and since I outranked the young Lieutenant, I strongly brought to his attention to the fact that I did not appreciate his not picking me up at the airport. He said, "Well it seems we have a little situation here."

I replied, "I don't want to hear about any situations - I've got business to take care of, and I also want to take our customary trip downtown to check out the cultural delights of the city."

Having made my point, I stowed my gear and we went out to the Jeep and headed downtown to our local haunts. I always enjoyed our rides through town because I was fascinated by the local culture, but today something seemed different. As we cruised down the avenue at a high rate of speed, I continued to notice the lack of the customary crowds. It was definitely a twilight zone moment.

Keep in mind Nakada had yet to mention there was a war going on downtown. As we were flying down the street we drove past some American combat troops who were frantically waving their arms, indicating that we should stop. Lt. Nakada continued past them at a high rate of speed, ignoring their signals. I felt that perhaps they were trying to tell us something, but Nakada motored on.

Suddenly we found ourselves in the middle of a war. There were opposing forces in buildings on either side of the street, shooting at each other. We had bullets flying across in front, behind, and above us. I screamed at Nakata, wondering what in the world had he gotten us into.

I looked over to see this strange grin on his face, as he gripped the wheel with both hands and kept barreling along. I suggested strongly that we get out of the area.

Since live fire was going on and there was no place to stop and make a U-turn, we followed the practice of driving through ambushes. Unless it was really bad, we had discovered from past experience it was best to drive through it like Richard Petty heading for a checkered flag. With much luck, we safely emerged from the active combat area and headed back to our relatively safe facilities at the depot office.

Back at the office we were safe because we were protected by Korean troops, and those guys definitely gave you a feeling of security. Then I asked Lt. Nakada if he was aware of the situation downtown. And with that same grin on his face, he said yes.

Then I asked him if he had a death wish for both of us. He laughed, until I said that he may get his wish soon since I felt like shooting him for taking me into that street battle.

We got over that fairly quickly, and were soon laughing about it. We were also chuckling at the Korean solution for clearing the bad guys out of the city of Qui Nhon.

Korean soldiers in Viet Nam were bad dudes, and I believe the only reason they were there was because we insisted they participate and help us, because we had come to their aid in the Korean War. There was little love lost on the Vietnamese by the Koreans. They had a job to do and aggressively pursued the issue in their areas of operations.

Initially, when the bad guys occupied downtown Qui Nhon, the Koreans were given the mission to clear the city, and their idea was a unique and effective method of accomplishing the mission.

They took about one hundred 106 recoilless rifles, which were highly lethal anti-tank guns mounted on Jeeps, and lined up them up hub to hub on the edge of town and began firing directly into the city. They would continue firing until everything in front of them was blown away. They knocked out everything in their path.

Then they would move that line of vehicles forward a few blocks and continue firing and killing everything in sight, including friendlies, buildings, dogs, water buffaloes, and everything else that got in their way. It proved to be a very effective strategy, however, it caused serious public relations difficulties with the locals.

After a short duration of this severe but effective tactic, the Koreans were relieved of their mission and sent back out to the hinterlands. American units were given the job to finish up clearing the city. That was done in a few more days.

After finishing my business at Qui Nhon, I moved inland over to Pleiku and then up to the city of Kon Tum, where I saw the results of the Tet Offensive. It gave me a heavy heart.

It appeared the intention of the northern invaders was to act as vandals rather than combat troops. At every town large and small I traveled through, it was apparent the northern troops were primarily interested in destroying the infrastructure of the South.

Everything they could get their grimy little hands on was destroyed, including stores, manufacturing facilities, homes, restaurants, gas stations, and whatever else they could devastate or damage. It looked like their idea was, if you don't come with us, you're not going to have anything. I saw many people homeless, miserable, or dead as a result of this cowardly campaign against the people of South Vietnam.

I learned something else about the big picture in world affairs in Tet of 68. My father had been a Sinclair Refining Company distributor as I was growing up, and I developed an interest in the petroleum business. In Vietnam they had three petroleum distributors – ESSO (Eastern States Standard Oil Co), Caltex (Standard Oil of California and Texaco), and Shell (Royal Dutch Shell of the Netherlands and Great Britian).

Before the Tet Offensive I marveled at how in a rather backward country with a war going on, all three of those companies maintained relatively stable and widespread operations.

Each company had their distinctively decorated gas stations scattered throughout the country and the stations were supplied by a fleet of delivery trucks painted in the respective company colors - Shell with its yellow, Caltex with its red, and ESSO with its white and blue.

I was dismayed and appalled when I witnessed the destruction of the gas stations across Vietnam. But I began to notice something very interesting. ESSO and Caltex assets suffered much damage, but the Shell Oil infrastructure showed little impairment and was operating as usual immediately after the Tet Offensive.

I was puzzled by this, wondering how the northern invaders could miss all the Shell stations. They were able to hit the Esso and Caltex stations and delivery trucks but somehow they seemed to overlook the yellow Shell stations and trucks.

Later a friend of mine who worked at the large petroleum terminal at Cam Ranh Bay explained the situation to me and I began to see the light. It seems the Royal Dutch Shell Oil Company had a large refinery down in Singapore and they had contracts with both the U.S. military and North Vietnam to supply petroleum products.

My friend told me tankers would regularly bring loads of refined petroleum out of Singapore and drop off half of the load at Cam Ranh Bay and take the other half up to Haiphong in the North.

Then it became crystal clear to me why Shell stations and trucks remained unharmed through the mayhem of the Tet Offensive. It was obvious the Royal Dutch Shell Oil Company was conducting their own brand of foreign policy.

I'm sure they informed the leaders in the North it would be to their detriment if Shell assets in the South suffered any great misfortunes during the Tet Offensive, because the leaders in the North valued a reliable source of critical fuel for their war activities.

The Tet Offensive of 1968 caused political ripples back in the USA, in addition to the destruction in Vietnam.

In most cases the opposing forces were quickly cleared out of the towns they invaded, except for the city of Hue, where there was a large old fortress. The US Marines were assigned the   mission of clearing Hue and got bogged down. The US Army's 1st Cavalry Division was called in and they made short work of eliminating the invaders. The 1st Cavalry Division was accustomed to helping the Marines since they also came to their rescue at the battle of Khe Sanh.

Unfortunately, many things changed forever for South Vietnam as a result of this hideous assault on the struggling nation.

7- More Third Brigade Adventures

Back at LZ Baldy things were a little quiet compared to what I had been through at Qui Nhon and over in the central Highlands. About the only effect it had on us at LZ Baldy was it gave everyone something to talk about. By the time I got back, the gravity of the situation was beginning to be realized by everyone, and we began to appreciate the historical nature of the event.

As actions were taken in response to the Tet Offensive, the U.S. Army felt its repercussions all over the world. This caused drastic actions in some cases.

One interesting example was the fact that even my old unit, the 82nd Airborne Division at Fort Bragg, North Carolina, was drawn into the affair. At that time the 82nd Airborne Division was America's first line of defense. Whenever anything happened around the world that needed combat troops in a hurry, the 82nd Airborne Division was on 24 hour alert to move out quickly to wherever the problem presented.

In this case the problem presenting was the Tet Offensive in Vietnam. Somewhere in the Pentagon someone apparently panicked and decided to send the 82nd Airborne Division to Vietnam to help with putting down the offensive.

As mentioned earlier, we had moved north a few miles above the city Chu Lai, which was also the headquarters for the Americal Division to which our provisional third brigade was attached. They were our supply source. So I had regular business at Chu Lai.

One day I happened to be there shortly after the cessation of the Tet Offensive hostilities. I espied a Jeep with bumper markings indicating it was from the 82nd Airborne Division. This was another twilight zone moment because I knew the 82nd Airborne Division should be at Fort Bragg, North Carolina, standing guard as America's first line of defense.

Later I confirmed with personnel at the Americal Division, those were in fact 82nd Airborne Division vehicles. The hearsay source told me that elements of the Division landed at their airport because the pilots of the transport planes bringing them to Vietnam had no instructions as to where to land. They just scattered out and landed at their choice of airports across the country. One brigade of the 82nd ended up at Chu Lai, apparently by happenstance.

And so a brigade of the 82nd Airborne Division was deposited at Chu Lai with the Americal Division with no specific instructions as to what their mission might be, other than a general directive to assist in combating the Tet Offensive.

I spoke with some of the members of the 82nd Airborne Division and many were in shock that they were in Vietnam. Several stated that they had just left Vietnam only weeks before. Other stated that they had no mission and were just camped out in any open space they could find near the airfield.

That was another lesson to me about Army planning. I reasoned either they don't have it all together, or maybe from my lowly position on the totem pole, I could not see the big picture. Little things like the 82nd Airborne Division unexpectedly showing up in Vietnam should not be a matter of concern to me.

I did have a nice time reminiscing with the boys from Fort Bragg about what was going on back in Fayetteville at the entertainment spots on Hay Street and Bragg Boulevard, and other happenings on the Cape Fear River.

As soon as the higher-ups were confident the Tet Offensive was under control, the 82nd was returned to their home at Fort Bragg to resume their duties as America's frontline guard of honor.

Things settled down after the Tet Offensive and life became rather routine at LZ Baldy. Luckily my job required me to make frequent trips away from the LZ to Chu Lai, Qui Nhon, and on occasion, back to the 4th Division at Pleiku.

One day I had the duty of escorting one of our S and P's (semi-trailer truck), which was returning a damaged piece of specialized equipment to the reclassification facility at Qui Nhon.

The few major highways in Vietnam were very busy with military traffic. Large convoys ran every day all over the country keeping the military units supplied, so anything getting in the way of these convoys was a serious concern and it was not something you would want to do.

Every day a 500 truck convoy ran on Highway 1. So here I was escorting the truck to Qui Nhon, heading south on Highway 1 just ahead of the daily 500 truck convoy. I was in a Jeep and being followed by the truck carrying the damaged equipment. We got an early start that day so we would not get tied up in the daily convoy.

So here I was, on my mission of escorting the truck down to Qui Nhon, heading south on Highway 1, the major North-South road in the country. I was in a Jeep and our truck was close behind. We got an early start that day so that we would not get tied up in the daily convoys.

Much to my dismay, just a few miles down the road, I looked back just as the driver of the truck lost control and went partially into the ditch and blocked the roadway. I knew that in a very short time a 500 truck convoy escorted by all sorts of armored vehicles with machine guns and 40 mm antiaircraft guns would appear and not be too happy about being stopped by a truck in the middle of the road.

Apparently one of the few attributes I possessed that kept me in the Army was the ability to think fast in tight situations. This was one of those situations that required lots of fast thinking.

My Jeep driver and I quickly returned to the wrecked vehicle and with the drivers attempted to right the truck, but to no avail. As the panic began to set in I had to think fast.

I knew I would be in deep trouble if it was reported that a Lt. Payne had disrupted a major supply route in Vietnam, so I wanted to do something fast.

I remembered a mile or so back we had passed a small armored unit firebase. I hopped in the Jeep and had the driver step on it, and we headed for that firebase. I instructed the driver that excessive speeds were authorized in this situation and we tore into that firebase in a cloud of dust and skidded to a stop.

I ran into what looked like a headquarters shack and explained my case and pleaded for their help. Initially they did not share my concern and commented on the fact that I had a problem. However, as all good salesman understand, I was not going to take no for an answer.

After a few minutes of begging, pleading, screaming, commanding and cajoling, they finally offered the only vehicle they had available - a massive M-88 tank retriever. Those vehicles are the largest tracked vehicles in the Army inventory. They make the ground rumble whenever they pass by. They're designed to pull disabled tanks and are extremely large vehicles.

I encouraged him to drive as fast as that hulking machine would go, and led the way back to our disabled vehicle. As I pulled back on the highway I could see the lead elements of the convoy heading our way.

I figured with an M-88 following me, I could hide from the convoy commanders. We rushed back to our vehicle as fast as that dinosaur of a vehicle could go. And of course with a vehicle that size, they quickly made short order of pulling our truck back on the highway.

After thanking them profusely and offering them everything I could think of, we said our goodbyes and took off for Qui Nhon. That was one of the few times in Vietnam I was really worried. The Vietcong and the NVA can be fearsome, but nothing is worse than an irate convoy commander leading 500 trucks.

After the truck was returned to the highway we took off and made it safely to Qui Nhon. We quickly unloaded the damaged equipment at the rehab facility and finished the paperwork.

Lt. Nakada, our liaison officer at Qui Nhon, needed to go to LZ Baldy for some reason, so he bummed a ride with us in the Jeep. This he would later come to regret.

As soon as we finished the administrative details and got Lt. Nakada loaded up, we headed back north as fast as we could go. I knew it was going to be difficult to make the long trip in one day, so I again authorized excessive speed to make sure we got back before dark.

You did not want to be driving around at night in Vietnam. It was highly recommended not to do such a thing, plus it was against regulations. Major highways like Highway 1 were barricaded at night with razor wire concertina.

The roads were guarded by the South Vietnamese Army at night, with particular attention paid to the bridges. The bad guys seemed to delight in destroying bridges so those long supply convoys would be delayed. It must have been awfully discouraging to the little guys because every time they would destroy a bridge, the Army Engineers would quickly repair the bridges and those 500 truck convoys would keep rolling everyday.

I definitely wanted to make it back to LZ Baldy and sleep in my humble cot that night. Unfortunately it looked like the day was going to run out on us before we made it back.

It was my wont to overlook regulations. I decided to take our chances and continue driving into the night. Shortly we would experience a spectacular event as we raced up Highway 1 in the late afternoon sun.

This particular event was without a doubt the most spectacular Jeep wreck to ever occur in the country. Unfortunately I must admit that I was at the wheel of the Jeep when it happened.

Against my better judgment I was pushing hard to get back to LZ Baldy before dark. I took over the driving duties because I did not feel the Jeep driver was capable of driving as fast as we needed to go.

As it got darker I began to drive faster and just as dusk was setting in it happened. At about 70 miles an hour I drove into a large hole in the road that apparently was the result of a mine or explosive charge having gone off.

The hole was almost large enough to swallow up the entire vehicle and I hit it on the left side. The Jeep was launched into the air and rotated 180 degrees clockwise while flying, and landed inverted in a dry rice paddy, about three feet below the road.

The strangest thing was all three occupants in the Jeep apparently were held into their seats by inertia. None of us were wearing seat belts. All three of us were uninjured other than being a little shaken up.

We crawled out of the overturned vehicle and wondered how we made it out alive. By this time the truck following behind had caught up with us and the drivers were stunned we were still alive because our wreck was so spectacular.

After cheating death, we checked out the Jeep and wondered what we were going to do because it was getting dark. Our distress was only heightened when the South Vietnamese guards on a nearby bridge suddenly opened up with everything they had, including hand grenades.

We took cover behind the overturned Jeep wondering if we had been spared death in the wreck only to be slaughtered by the Viet Cong. They weren't shooting at us, so we decided to leave the area ASAP.

We flipped the Jeep back over right side up, checked it out, and much to our surprise it had very little damage and the motor came to life. So just like Dale Earnhardt who once continued to race a car that had flipped over, I figured, why not? Let's hop in and go.

Apparently Lt. Nakada was either in a state of shock or suffering from a slight concussion because he was acting strange. His helmet had been bent inward on one side. I fired up the Jeep and told the driver and Lt. Nakada to get in. Lt. Nakada stumbled into the Jeep and tried to put his helmet on and noticed it was mashed in on one side. Despite the damage he tried to fit it on his head, but was unaware it was full of sand. When he attempted to put the helmet on, the sand came out and covered him with the grit. The driver and I got a big laugh out of the sight, despite our efforts to not make him feel any worse.

By the time we finished our little exercise with the Jeep it was dark and the roads were closed, but we were able to convince the trigger-happy South Vietnamese bridge guards to let us through. There was a small firebase installation not far away and we made it there and spent the night in the middle of a truck park. It was a little uncomfortable but at least it was secure and there were no Vietnamese bridge guards throwing hand grenades our way.

The next morning we arose and continued to our home at LZ Baldy. My Jeep ran well but it was a little beat up, and unfortunately when we got back, some local scavengers decided to strip the vehicle.

The rest of our two-month stay at LZ Baldy passed without much excitement, and then we received word we were moving to a firebase near Bong Son.

Bong Son was a nice little village about 40 miles north of Qui Nhon on Highway 1. I had spent two months with the third brigade at Duc Pho, then two months at LZ Baldy, and now I was to spend two months with the Third Brigade at Bong Son.

For us in the Third Brigade S&T Company (Provisional), life was rather mundane during our two months at Bong Son except for the fact we were situated immediately adjacent to a South Vietnamese 155 mm artillery battery.

I had already noted that the South Vietnamese were a little lax in their attention to proper military procedures and this situation solidified that opinion. With American artillery units there are certain safety protocols that are strictly adhered to during firing. One is something called Min QE (minimum quadrant elevation).

Min QE simply means, the lowest allowable angle artillery tubes are only allowed to be fired as determined by local safety considerations. Apparently the South Vietnamese artillerymen either were unaware of Min QE procedures or they simply disregarded such inconveniences.

Our company location was mere yards from the South Vietnamese artillery tubes and they displayed absolutely no regard for min QE's. Frequently they would fire their cannons directly over our company area at dangerously low angles.

A person walking across our company area when a volley was fired at low angles would literally be lifted off the ground 12 inches. It would also stir up lots of dust, which meant we were always dusty and dirty. That was one of the aspects of life at Bong Son that comes to mind.

Another interesting memory of Bong Son regards the leadership of the provisional support battalion. The original Battalion Commander rotated back home and was replaced with another less than stellar Commander. He distinguished himself primarily by having the ability to levitate himself up and down vertically in his chair any time he was confronted with bad news.

He was not nearly as effective as his predecessor but he did provide a few laughs for anyone observing him bouncing up and down in his chair. The mirth was short lived though because things were winding down for the Provisional Third Brigade.

Word had come down that the Third Brigade - Provisional was going to disband and all its elements would return to the operational control of the 4th Division at Pleiku. Now I would have the pleasure of returning to the company of Col. Pond Scum, who still commanded the 4th S&T Battalion.

Something had happened earlier that set into motion an ominous chain of events that would present me with a significant challenge. leading to some very mysterious outcomes.

8 -They Picked on the Wrong Boy

While we were still at LZ Baldy I was given the lofty title of Brigade Supply Officer when the previous holder of that distinguished title rotated back to the States. The first thing I wanted to know when I was assigned to that job was exactly what was a brigade supply officer?

I found out the brigade supply officer is the official charged with the administration of all supply requests for the brigade. That person insures all requisitions are properly submitted and the requested material is properly received and accounted for.

Sounded pretty simple so I figured, no problem I can handle the job. After digging into the brigade supply records I began to discover that proper record procedures were not used by the previous administration.

This was mid 1968 and it was right at the end of what I call the "Wild West" days of the Vietnam War. They began when the Army first arrived en masse during 1965 and 1966, and gradually came to a close in mid-1968.

In the Wild West days it was apparent that the tactical mission took precedence over paperwork and other assorted administrative duties. Upon arrival at the Third Brigade Provisional at Duc Pho, I was rather surprised at the lax supply procedures used to obtain necessary supplies for the brigade.

In some cases proper requisitions were submitted for needed items and in other cases the tactical mission came first. On occasion our liaison officer at the depot would spray paint our brigade ID number on the desired item. A truck would be sent to pick up "our" item because it had our ID number on it.

That system did not adhere to established Army procedures but it works quite well in a tactical environment where life and death is at stake.

After assuming the office of brigade supply officer and making a cursory inspection of the records, I realized they would never stand up to an IG inspection. I had attended the Army Supply Officers Management Course at Fort Lee, Virginia just prior to my assignment to Vietnam. You could easily see the supply records of the Third Brigade were for all intents and purposes, drastically incomplete.

After discussing the matter with my superiors it was understood that the situation had been created as a result of tactical considerations rather than incompetence or malfeasance on the part of anyone involved.

My decision was to carry on and make sure the brigade got everything it needed in the way of logistics. I saluted with my best U-boat commander open finger style and carried on.

We moved down to Bong Son and after two months the Third Brigade Provisional was relocated to the division headquarters and dissolved as a separate unit.

Earlier I described the 4th S&T Battalion commander back at Camp Enari whom I referred to as Col. Pond Scum. I described him as a lopsided crusader obsessed with insuring every officer in the Army performed up to his high standards of conduct. I still remember the sad case of the young officer who got in trouble managing the Post Exchange and how Col. Pond Scum publicly humiliated him at the Lieutenant's going away party.

Shortly before we were to break camp at Bong Son and return to the Division headquarters at Pleiku. I received a visit from two of Col. Pond Scum's emissaries. They informed me since the Third Brigade Provisional and the Third Brigade Support Battalion, also Provisional, were shutting down, I would be responsible as the brigade supply officer for accounting for all the logistical supplies the Brigade had received since its arrival in country.

I mistakenly assumed these emissaries were reasonable individuals and would understand the situation that had developed over the years out here at the Brigade Supply Office of the Third Brigade.

Unfortunately, I quickly discovered they did not accept the explanation that the lack of complete records at the brigade supply office was due to active war time activities. I was informed by these emissaries that Col. Pond Scum was going to require me to account for every supply acquisition by the brigade since it had first arrived in Vietnam. He was intent on ferreting out all the misconduct he perceived at the Brigade Supply Office. He was driven to punish all those responsible to the fullest extent. Putting it bluntly, the man was an idiot.

The emissaries informed me that since I was the current brigade supply officer I would be held responsible for any and all unaccountable items. I immediately informed these messengers that would be impossible since to the best of my knowledge the records did not exist.

They informed me that Col. Pond Scum intended to initiate an Article 32 investigation. In civilian terms that is the equivalent to a grand jury investigation. And furthermore, if the investigation discovered I could not account for all the equipment received by the brigade, I would be charged with gross misconduct of duty and placed before a general court-martial due to the anticipated amount of money involved.

This was a sample of how Col. Pond Scum reacted to perceived misconduct of any officer in his command. Unfortunately for Col. Pond Scum, he picked on the wrong boy this time.

Initially when I was informed of his intentions, I was confident cooler heads would prevail because the situation was obvious. There was no theft going on. We were fighting a war and sometimes maintenance of administrative records took a back seat to winning the war. But Col. Pond Scum was fighting his own war and he pushed the issue relentlessly.

The time to pack our bags and equipment and return to Pleiku came as I continued to plead my case, but it was to no avail against the assault the self-righteous Col. was directing my way.

I had confidence throughout the affair that my special guardian angel was watching over me. This confidence came from the many "Indiana Jones" type events I had experienced in my life where there were so many near misses. I even named him Gabriel. And apparently Gabriel was with me during this ordeal.

I will swear on a stack of Bibles that I had nothing to do with the events that unfolded in the next few weeks. And besides, I think the statute of limitations has run out by now so you'll have to make up your own mind as to any involvement on my part.

By the time we got ready to pack up at Bong Son and head back to Pleiku. I had already been involved in much heated debate and discussion on this matter. The more we talked, the more Col. Pond Scum dug in his heels on the issue. I was beginning to get a little miffed.

I was just a country boy who grew up outside of Ocala, Florida, who was trying to do my job and I refused to let some misguided wacko cause me any discomfort.

The day finally came to leave peaceful Bong Son. We were being replaced by the 173rd Airborne Brigade and they had arrived. It was time for us to go and face the challenges ahead.

The route back to Camp Enari and the 4th Division was down Highway 1 to Highway 19, where we hung a right and headed for the mountains of the Central Highlands.

The brigade supply office records we did have were very important and I made sure we carefully packed them all on one specially selected vehicle.

I was delayed a few hours and did not move out with the main convoy. I departed later in my Jeep, along with the truck loaded with our brigade supply office records and other important items.

I always enjoyed the drive on Highway 19 into the Central Highlands because it was an exciting adventure for a Florida flatlander. It would start at Highway 1 in the coastal lowlands and then as we proceeded west on the 80 mile trip to Pleiku, we would have to negotiate two passes. One was the An Khe Pass and the other was the more dangerous Man Yang (sic) Pass.

As our little two-vehicle convoy was rushing to catch up with the main convoy, we experienced a terrible accident. As we were making our way through the Man Yang Pass we lost the truck with the brigade supply office records. Luckily the drivers survived but the truck went over a steep cliff and fell hundreds of feet to the valley below.

It was a spectacular accident, just like you would see in a James Bond movie. Apparently in addition to the records, the vehicle contained enough accelerants to cause it to be immediately engulfed in flames and burn to the frame.

So all we could do was collect the truck drivers in our Jeep and head west. We arrived safely back at Camp Enari, even though we had driven in a lone Jeep over one of the most dangerous stretches of highway in Vietnam.

And would you believe, Colonel Pond Scum was waiting at the vehicle park to welcome me back? He immediately inspected my vehicle and trailer and confiscated my personal AK-47, saying it was unauthorized, despite the fact everyone and his brother in Vietnam had an AK-47. They were just a cool weapon and it was well-known the standard issue M-16 was not worth the plastic it was made from.

Col. Pond Scum was very distressed to learn we had lost a vehicle on our trip back to the base camp. I really wasn't too worried about it because I had seen about 5000 of the exact same vehicles in the storage yards back at Qui Nhon.

Col. Pond Scum was a despicable, round-faced, bald headed individual. His round bald head had the tendency to turn red when he got upset and he was very red when he heard that all the brigade supply office records were destroyed in that unfortunate accident. And this seemed only to increase his vigor in pursuing the matter.

After getting settled in the base camp at Pleiku, the investigation into the Third Brigade Provisional Brigade Supply Office status continued. I was informed by many of the officers involved in the investigation that they agreed with me that it was much ado about nothing, however Colonel Pond Scum was intent on pushing the matter.

The Article 32 investigation was begun and things did not look good. As you know, attorneys can be very persuasive as they advocate a particular side of a question. I was being painted as a big-time embezzler because there were no records to show the proper disposition of all that matériel the Third Brigade had received.

I never really worried much about the outcome of the situation due to my confidence in Gabriel's ability to always come through and help me whenever I really needed it.

True to form, I was saved from a distressful situation by mysterious events. The episode ended well for me, but not so for the Col.

An amazing thing happened just as Col. Pond Scum was preparing to file a general court-martial, charging me with all sorts of terrible things. He unfortunately came down with a severe case of hepatitis. It was so severe they had to send him back to the States. When he left, sanity prevailed and all motivation for pursuing my court-martial evaporated immediately.

The entire matter was disposed of in file 13, as it should have been from the very beginning. We were fighting a war against a real live enemy and looking for unreasonable infractions for the purpose of crucifying officers was a gross waste of time, energy, and assets.

No comment as to how Col. Pond Scum came down with such a serious case of hepatitis. I do not wish the man any harm but I did not shed any tears as they hauled his worthless carcass away.

As this episode of my Vietnam adventures closed the next one opened, as I began my return engagement at the 4th Division base camp at Pleiku. Honestly, I much preferred being back out in the woods at the forward bases as opposed to the division base camp, despite its superior creature comforts.

9 - Back at Camp Enari

After Col. Pond Scum was medevaced due to his severe case of hepatitis, a new Battalion Commander came in who was a big improvement over his predecessor. The tension level around the battalion area was reduced significantly when we did not have to worry about such things as being court-martialed for walking on the grass. One of the guys set up a huge croquet field on the previously taboo grassy area. Many took up the game just to enjoy walking on the grass.

So now it was time to settle into my new mundane job in the Division Supply Office. It was a real live desk job which I was not in love with, but in the Army you do what they tell you, to the best of your abilities. I have to say it was a real challenge to sit at a desk all day and look for something to do so as to appear busy, while there was a real live a war going on nearby.

I greatly missed all my traveling adventures with the Third Brigade because now I was desk-bound, except for the occasional recon expeditions. Since I had already been out on a few of those walks through the woods, I was now allowed to lead my own expeditions out in the AO.

I enjoyed these recon missions for the most part. They generally lasted three days, which necessitated spending two nights out in the woods sleeping under the stars.

One of the biggest challenges of leading one of these recon missions was that the only personnel the units would provide were not the cream of the crop. It was the perfect place to send screw-ups they wanted to be rid of for a few days. It didn't seem to matter that they generally caused challenges for the patrol leader.

My fellow patrol leaders did not help the situation with some of the things they would pull. The procedure for these patrols was to be dropped off at a location, then you would go out on a route provided by the Division Base Security Office.

These routes were supposedly carefully designed to provide the division with accurate information about areas of interest in the Division's security zone.

The routes provided would generally take us on a 10 to 12 mile march through the woods, up and down the hills, across the creeks and then back to a pickup point. Of course this is hearsay, but it was reported to me some of the officers who led these patrols were not very scrupulous about following the assigned route. Some of the patrol leaders would dismount the truck at the drop off point and move to the vicinity of the pickup point where they would camp out until the trucks came to pick them up.

I would always follow the route as provided in the instructions. Unfortunately this riled up some of the regular patrol members. On more than one occasion I was presented with rather challenging discipline problems from some of the super troopers who did not relish the thought of actually following the assigned route through the woods and up and down the hills and across the creeks.

I insisted we follow the routes because not only could we see the interesting sights along the way, we might also actually run into some bad guys and have some fun.

There was one occasion where I got into a little hot water as a result of conflicts with the recon patrol super troopers. One of the biggest complainers would not shut up and complained over and over about how I was such a bad guy who made them actually follow the route, and it got so bad he refused to continue on our mission.

We were way out in the woods and I informed him he had the choice to either come with us or he could stay there. We moved out and he elected to stay. I figured he would have a change of heart and catch up with us but he didn't. We proceeded on without him. We got back to the pickup point and he never showed up. When the trucks came we loaded up and went back to the base camp. Unfortunately I got into hot water with the higher-ups for leaving him out in the woods alone. We had to make a special trip back to the woods to retrieve the young lad.

Other than the occasional patrol adventure, life was calm back at the Division Base Camp, except for the occasional rocket attack. Every once in a while the opposing forces would provide us with a little diversion by firing 122 mm rockets into the base camp. Now keep in mind the Camp Enari Base Camp was over 2 square miles in area and a few stray rockets flying in very seldom if ever did any significant damage.

I enjoyed the commotion and secretly looked forward to the next time we would have a rocket attack. Those motorized bombs sounded like the Orange Blossom Special when they would come flying over and it was really exciting if one would land close enough that you could feel the impact.

But not to worry, the base camp was very well protected against such attacks and we had very substantial bunkers that would withstand direct hits from these highly unreliable devices. Unlike all the smart bombs of today, these were rather dumb. These type weapons were aimed and fired with a hope and promise they would hit something.

We did not receive that many rocket attacks at the base camp during my tenure. I was impressed by the fact that in spite of all the noise, they did very little damage. It was a case of luck and proper preparation.

It must have been very frustrating to the little guys in the opposing forces. There was such minor damage being done despite all the work they had to do to lug those rockets overland from the Ho Chi Minh trail so they could fire them into the 4th Infantry Division's base camp.

Another advantage of living back at the base camp was they had better and more live entertainment - specifically, many live bands from the Subic Bay in the Philippines. I will always remember the announcers proclaiming this was a hot band from Subic Bay. I always figured Subic Bay must be the Nashville of the Philippines.

Those bands would regale us with the old favorites like: "We Gotta Get Out Of This Place," "If You Are Going To San Francisco," and "Give Me A Ticket For An Airplane." Out at the forward bases all we ever got were movies and ice cream.

Occasionally I would be offered an opportunity to interrupt my monotonous existence in the Division Supply Office. The most notable experience came when

I was selected to lead a detail on a resupply mission at a Special Forces Camp at Dak Seang.

You may remember when I first arrived at the 4th Infantry Division, our one-week orientation class was curtailed by an ongoing battle at Dak To. It was a little village north of Kon Tum near the tri-border area. In late 1967 the bad guys assembled about 12,000 troops around Dak To with the intention of wiping out a small force of 4th Division troops stationed there.

It grew into a serious battle where not only did the 4th Division participate, but they were joined by elements of the 173rd Airborne Brigade and the 1st Cavalry Division. They had a hellacious battle for several weeks. The US forces lost about 300 soldiers and the opposition lost around 3000.

It ended as most battles did over there. The bad guys would make a stand somewhere and they would get the hell beat out of them and then they would withdraw after doing as much damage as they could. In most cases they always came out on the short end of the stick.

When I went to Dak Seang with my detachment of soldiers it was in support of operations in the Dak To area. Our mission there was to rig air-dropped supplies from C-130s so they could be moved to Dak To with helicopters.

It was a rewarding experience because we were busy and there was a tangible benefit to the work we were doing. We were housed at a Special Forces camp. It was always interesting to be around these SF guys because they always had interesting stories to tell.

There was also a large force of Montenyards at the camp. Montenyards were native tribesmen living in the mountains who hired out as mercenaries to the Special Forces. The Montenyard soldiers brought their families with them, so in addition to the Special Forces, there was a large group of mercenaries and their families at the camp.

Dak Seang was a very interesting place. It was near to where the borders of Vietnam, Laos and Cambodia came together, which put us in close proximately to the Ho Chi Minh Trail. Even though it was high in the mountains, it was the hottest place I've ever been. At one point I thought I was going to die of heat exhaustion. Luckily the SF guys had many of the comforts of home and we had plenty of cold water to drink.

It was also the loneliest place I've ever been. Other than the the Special Forces camp, there was no sign of humanity anywhere as far as you could see. That's why I was so puzzled one day when I was out on the drop zone and suddenly I heard the Rolling Stones singing "I Can't Get No Satisfaction."

I was wondering if I was losing it when I heard the Rolling Stones, because we had no radios or tape players with us. I discovered the music was coming from a group of Montenyards who had been down to the creek. As they walked by, one was carrying a large boom box on his shoulder just like someone in the "hood" back home. I was relieved to learn where it was coming from.

Something else very unusual happened at Dak Seang. One day as we were rigging loads, a Huey helicopter landed and my cousin, Major Guy H. Payne from Ozark, Alabama hopped out. He was in the Engineers and was checking on something.

It was a big surprise to see my cousin from Ozark, Alabama at Dak Seang in Vietnam. We had a little chat and then he got down to business, ensuring we were doing our job correctly. He departed and I was not to see him again until we met at the store in Skipperville, Alabama years later.

My guardian angel, Gabriel, was at work again. In a few weeks our mission was complete at Dak Seang and we returned to the base camp at Pleiku. I had noticed the building where I was sleeping was made of concrete blocks with a stucco covering. I also noticed that there were sections of the stucco on the wall that had been repaired.

At first I saw it on the inside, and then I went outside and realized the building had lots of gunfire damage that had been repaired. I figured this little outpost had seen its share of hostile activity.

For that reason I was not sad to leave, considering we were in a very isolated position with a small number of personnel, and not very far from the Ho Chi Minh Trail.

I was very happy when the aircraft came and took us away. It was a relief to get back to the security of Camp Enari. It turned out to be a well-founded concern. A few days after our return we heard the North Vietnamese Army attacked the camp the day following our departure. It was reported the NVA attacked with tanks, destroyed the camp and killed all the Special Forces personnel, plus many of the Montenyards. The surviving Montenyards escaped into the mountains.

Had we stayed another night I am afraid we would have suffered the same fate as the SF guys. Again, I was thankful to my guardian angel, Gabriel, for his protection.

After enduring a few weeks in the Division Supply Office I was assigned as commander of the 4th S&T Battalion, Headquarters Company. I was happy about this for two reasons: one, it got me out of the Division Supply Office and it is always good for officers to log time in command slots, and two, I always like to be in charge.

While I was the Headquarters Company Commander we had an event that convinced me I would never be a drug user. The division commander decided it would be a good idea for everybody in the base camp to go out on a massive reconnaissance sweep of the division security area. It was a circular area around the base camp with a 10 mile radius.

The plan was to turn out everybody in the base camp, including everyone from mechanics to clerks. Only a few fire guards remained in camp. Everybody would go out and side-by-side march out from the base camp and sweep away everything in our front.

As you can imagine it was a big project and rather difficult to control. Maneuvering large bodies of troops trained for such operations is no easy task but if you get hundreds of desk jockeys out into the bushes it's even more difficult.

Okay, so how do the drugs fit into this picture? The operation began. The troops from my headquarters company were lined up as directed and as we moved forward, it was a continuous stop and start thing because there was great difficulty in maintaining the line as we moved outward from the base camp.

It involved many stops and starts and radio conversations with the higher-ups. I had a tendency to kneel down on one knee when the conversations would go for long periods. That would be followed by rising and walking a short distance and stopping for another radio conversation and kneeling down on one knee.

After a while the knee I used to kneel on began to hurt. The company medic was moving with me and the company first sergeant. I mentioned my knee was hurting from kneeling down so much and the medic offered me a pill, saying, "take this and it will help your knee." I asked what it was and he said it was Darvon.

I trusted his judgment and took the pill. Within a few minutes my knee stopped hurting, and not only that, I began to feel better - almost mellow. I began to lose my exasperation at the raggedness of the operation.

As we moved along I thought, if one pill made me feel that good, two pills should make me feel even better. So I asked the friendly medic for another Darvon pill, which he gladly supplied. It worked; I did feel better and my knee no longer hurt at all. As we continued walking through the woods, I figured a third pill would make me feel even better. The medic was more than happy to provide me with another pill. After about five pills nothing was bothering me and everything seemed nice.

Finally at the end of the day, we completed our mission and the division's area had been secured by this massive clearing operation. We returned to the base camp and I had a very pleasant sleep that night. However, the next morning at the required morning breakfast assembly for all officers, I was in bad shape. I was having a Darvon hangover that was so bad I swore off ever taking another drug unless I had a serious medical situation.

By the way, lucky for us we did not encounter any bad guys on that sweep.

10 - Snake Stories

My snake memoirs are placed here in their own separate chapter because in the words of that other famous adventurer, Huckleberry Finn, "I do not love snakes." As a matter of fact I hate snakes. There will be three snake stories given in this chapter. One is from my personal experience, which to this day gives me chills up my spine when I think about it. Another is from a rather humouous incident happening at Duc Pho and the third story was related to me by Cary D. Allen, a fellow officer in the 4th Infantry Division and one of the finest officers ever to pull on a pair of combat boots. I am confident Allen's story is accurate and true.

One of the things that impressed me about this far away and exotic land was the variety of animals found there. It was almost like Noah's Ark had unloaded in Vietnam. You could stock a good-sized zoo with the animals found there.

They had elephants, tigers, orangutans, moose, deer, and antelopes of all sizes to name a few, and those were just the mammals. They also had an interesting variety of all sorts are creepy crawly things.

My first story about snakes involves bamboo vipers and it occurred after I had returned to the base camp at Pleiku, and was still going out on our recon patrols.

So there we were, I and my trusty squad of recon troops, hiking across the western highlands of Vietnam. I had remained true to my infantry training by requiring the squad to maintain a proper tactical formation while moving through hostile territory.

The instructors at the Infantry School of Fort Benning would have been proud of the formation we were maintaining as we moved up and down the hilly terrain. I had flank guards out on both sides, I had the rear security out, and the point man was out front to give us any advance warnings of trouble. The sergeant and radio operator were with me. We were cruising along just like in a training film.

It was another one of those hot days that gave you a strong desire to jump into a cool swimming pool. We had been crossing a large open area with little shade to give us the slightest relief from the oppressive heat.

It was about time for a break so I indicated to our point man to head for a nearby bamboo grove. He headed in that direction and as he neared the bamboo he stopped and did not move.

Earlier I related to the reader that many of the men chosen to go out on these patrols were generally not the sharpest nails in the box. So I figured maybe our reluctant scout couldn't figure out what I wanted him to do. He was about 50 yards in front of the main body.

All my efforts to signal him to move into the grove did not work and he continued to stand in one spot, looking straight ahead. Being slightly perturbed at his failure to comply with my signals, I moved forward to inquire as to what the problem was.

I reached him and walked around to his front and he had a dazed look on his face. Keeping in mind he had been standing there for several minutes not moving, I asked if there was a problem and all he did was hold up a finger and slowly point it forward. I was facing him at that moment so I turned around to look at what he was pointing toward.

Suddenly I became well aware of what was causing his reticence to move forward. We were standing about four feet away from a large growth of bamboo and right there at eye height was the largest snake I had ever seen close-up, winding its way back into the bamboo.

For a moment, I was as shocked as the intrepid scout. Very carefully the scout and I slowly backed away from that monstrous reptile in the bamboo. If my memory serves me correctly the beast was six inches in diameter and I did not wait around to ascertain its length.

I continued backing up to regain my composure. My normal reaction to snakes is to shoot them. But considering where we were at the time, I did not want to call attention to our location. There could have been hostiles in the vicinity.

After a few moments passed, I had regained enough of my composure to utter a command to the squad. I decided that it would be safe to make a wide path around that evil looking reptile and move further away into the bamboo grove for respite from the oppressive heat.

We moved on a wide path of about 50 feet around the spot where that incredible beast had been spotted. And as we began to enter the grove there appeared directly in our path another reptile slowly weaving its way to our left on the ground. This reptilian monstrosity was at least 20 feet long and six inches in diameter and if I am lying I am dying.

This sighting was another blow to my composure that had only slightly recovered from my previous encounter.

We just stood in place watching this devilish creature pass by, as we all hoped it would leave and not bother us anymore. We gave the snake plenty of time to depart the area. After a few minutes I figured that had to be all the snakes we would encounter that day. I gave the order to move into the grove and take a break in the welcome shade.

As we moved into the grove I was surprised by another hideous monster of a snake in the bamboo. By this time my nerves were shot by the three snakes. I could handle attacks by men all day but the snakes had done me in.

I had had enough of bamboo groves. Even if they had been air-conditioned and supplied with a cool swimming pool I decided to do without the shade in that bamboo groove.

I never definitely confirmed what type snakes they were but I assumed since they were in bamboo they must have been bamboo vipers. I remember in the safety briefings we were always cautioned to be watchful of bamboo vipers because their venom was highly toxic and being bitten by one would cause severe injury or death. I had been referring to these snakes as bamboo vipers but after looking into the matter later I believe they were of some type of python or boa variety.

The peril of such reptiles is one of the reasons I was glad I was not a line doggie. Those poor guys had to put up with such things, in addition to bullets and bombs all the time.

Another common snake found in Vietnam was the King Cobra. I assume since there were so many in India it was easy for them to migrate over to the lush mountains and jungles of the Indo-Chinese Peninsula.

My good friend Cary D. Allen, a good old boy from Alabama and also one of the finest officers I had ever known in the Army, related to me a rather humorous snake story. It happened when he was assigned to one of the infantry units in the 4th Division.

This incident happened in the summer of 1967. Cary's unit was engaged in a heavy firefight with the enemy. It was intense, with both sides throwing everything they had at each other. The terrain was the typical rolling hills of the Central Highlands.

Suddenly the firing began to stop and Cary was not sure as to the cause of the cessation of firing. Suddenly it appeared, the large head of a King Cobra, fully fanned out about three feet above the ground. The snake was casually moving across the battle area.

It was estimated to be 10 to 15 feet long and seemed to be totally oblivious to the bedlam it was moving through.

Eventually all firing subsided as everyone on both sides of the battle stopped to watch this monstrous snake moving through the area with regal aplomb. A few moments after the hideous monster cleared the area the fighting renewed to its original level, as if nothing had happened.

The battle was put on hold so the monstrous King Cobra could pass by. It was never to be seen again.

Another interesting snake incident involved my good buddy Lt. Nakada. One night while we were at Duc Pho watching a movie outdoors in the company formation area it happened. It was a wonderful evening with gentle zephrs coming in off the South China Sea. Lt. Nakada liked to watch the movies in a relaxed manner. He would take off his shirt and boots and settle into a comfortable beach chair with rubber flip-flop sandals on his feet.

I was engrossed in watching the movie and did not notice him step away. Suddenly there was a commotion in the rear but the movie was too interesting for me to go and investigate. Shortly, someone reported Lt. Nakada had been bitten by a snake at the piss tube. I thought to myself "that's too bad" and continued watching the movie.

When the movie was over I figured it would be appropriate to inquire as to my buddy's condition after his snake bite. He had been taken over to the Brigad aid station where they sew up the wounded.

Upon hearing that news I summoned my driver and we rushed over to the Mini-MASH aid station. I walked into the operating section of the tent and noticed a curious scene.

On one operating table I saw Lt. Nakada lying on his back in obvious pain with several medical technicans working on his big toe. On an adjacent table there was our company first sergeant lying on his back also in obvious pain with several medical technicans feverously working on his big toe.

My first thought was a herd of snakes had invaded our company area and was attacking everyone wearing flip-flops. I was happy I always wore my jungle boots. You would never find Mrs. Payne's young son walking around barefooted in such a strange place.

I was perplexed at the sight in the aid station. It was a relief to learn the first sergeant's wound was a ripped toenail incurred as he was rushing around in the dark getting Lt. Nakada off to the aid station.

It was admirable on their parts all that went on without disturbing the movie.

11 - Goin' Home

Did you ever intensely think of something you really wanted every day for a whole year? When you were in Vietnam you knew the exact day you were going home and it was something you thought about constantly. There was no way you could make the time go faster or slower. In military lingo that day was called your DEROS day. If I am not mistaken that acronym meant "date of effective rotation from overseas." To anyone in Vietnam it was the sweetest word in the English language.

As your DEROS date grew closer there was a tendency to become happier and more cautious at the same time. On the one hand you were happy about going home and on the other hand, you did not want something to happen right at the end of your tour.

My last few months with the 4th S&T Battalion at the base camp of the 4th Infantry Division were spent as the Commander Of The Headquarters And Headquarters Company. Things were becoming a little more organized, so much of my time was spent on important things like inspections of the billets and weapons, and the occasional training class.

Unfortunately, even though that job had some career benefits, I missed the adventures of being on the road and seeing the Asian culture up close, and I actually enjoyed going out on the walks through the woods.

As with a pattern that had developed in my life, everything seems to happen to me at the beginning or end of life phases. If you remember in an earlier chapter I described how on my orientation patrol we happened to encounter members of the opposition and were engaged in a little gun battle in the woods.

I should have been on guard because on my last recon patrol, I encountered another interesting event. I had lucked out on all my previous recon patrols and never encountered rain while walking through the woods.

Apparently the rain gods saved up everything for my last patrol and unleashed something similar to the second flood on us. After two days of walking up and down the hills and dales in a heavy downpour, we were soaking wet and miserable. I had never seen the skin on my hands so wrinkled.

On the final night of the patrol, because it was so miserable, I relented and allowed the guys to break out their air mattresses for a little comfort and protection from the standing water on the ground.

I became a little disturbed as everyone took out their air mattresses, inflated them to the max, and settled in on them. It began to sound like the camp fire scene in the movie Blazing Saddles. You could hear the bodies rubbing on air mattresses even above the rain that was falling on us.

We did not realize at the time, probably because of the heavy downpour, we had set up relatively close to an RFPF position. RFPF's were something like our National Guard.

Suddenly in the middle of the night, all hell broke loose at the RFPF location. There was all sorts of small arms fire, and machine gun and hand grenade activity going on in their direction.

We were so miserable that night I made the decision to assume it was a typical false alarm as the RFPF forces were wont to commit. The firing died down and luckily our uncomfortable slumber was not disturbed the rest of that miserable night. But I figured it was par for the course since it was my last patrol. I knew very shortly I would be living the life of Riley as the Commander of Headquarters & Headquarters Company.

Another bit of excitement during the final days of my first year in Vietnam was the death of Martin Luther King. It caused a lot of trouble back in the States, with riots and all sorts of disturbances. Even the far-off country of Vietnam was not immune to reactions to the assignation.

There were rumors that in some locations down south there were riots, and in some cases buildings were set aflame. Many of the black soldiers in the 4th Division were enraged at this senseless act against a great American. Fortunately there were no riots at Camp Enari – just rage at the terrible act.

My replacement company commander came in about two weeks before I left, so I had the pleasure of watching him manage the difficult situation caused by the King assassination.

I do not remember the new commander's name but I do remember his policies. He was what you call a "hard ass" and as usual when a new hard ass guy comes in, he has to make sure everybody is in line. Unfortunately he came on board at the height of the Martin Luther King reactions. And all I can say is, I'm glad I was leaving.

My command philosophy was always to lead rather than to coerce and push. But that was the good thing about the Army; it was up to each commander to choose his own leadership style as long as he got the job done.

Finally that wonderful day came when it was my time to go home, a day that I had been thinking about intently for the previous 364 days, and for the first time I discovered how it felt to walk on air.

As it turned out my departure route followed the same path that brought me to Camp Enari. The day before my departure I packed up all the things I figured I could get through customs and inspections. Everything else was left in the walls of the BOQ (bachelor officer's quarters). There was nothing illegal, only such things as AK-47s, knives, ammo and such.

And finally that glorious day came and we were taken up to the airport at Pleiku where we boarded a C-130 and flew down to Cam Ranh Bay, to the very same replacement detachment we had walked through 365 days before. This time I had a much more relaxed attitude, although it was still in the back of my mind a dirty, nasty little Vietcong might run in and toss a satchel charge and kill us all just as we were leaving the country.

Luckily that did not happen. As soon as we arrived they herded us into a large room and gave us our instructions. For some reason they did not have an aircraft sitting on the runway ready to take us away immediately. We were told that we may have to stay there up to two days. In the meantime, I was able to loll around the club and await my name to be called on the loudspeaker.

Finally the appointed time came and we all assembled back in the same large room with our baggage where we were briefed on procedures. We then proceeded to those wonderful olive green buses that took us down to that beautiful Boeing 707.

As we loaded the bus I was happy and excited but at the same time subdued. I was still in a country where you could be blown up at any time or place. The buses slowly went down the winding road to the runway. The excitement level rose as we arrived at the airport and could see that big iron bird sitting there waiting on us. That big iron bird was going to take us back to the "world."

Slowly we loaded on the airplane in what seemed like an eternity. The flight personnel appeared to be moving in slow motion because we were all in a hurry to get out of that place. It remained quiet and subdued as we found our seats.

Finally after what felt like forever, the doors were closed, the stairs were pulled away, and the engines came to life. Still, every soldier on that plane sat motionless in silent anticipation, knowing that at any minute the plane could be destroyed by rocket fire or sappers.

Much to my appreciation the pilots of that 707 did not handle the plane as they would have at a civilian airport. These dudes must have shared our desire to get out of that place in a hurry.

Once the plane started to taxi toward the runway it moved along at a rapid clip. To get to the main runway they had to make two 90° turns and there was none of this stopping and starting; these boys hit those corners at maximum possible speed. It looked like the wing tips were going to scrape the ground they turned so fast.

The plane positioned for takeoff and there was no delay as is common at a civilian airport. As soon as that aircraft was lined up on the runway, the pilot hit the throttles with everything he had and powered down the runway as fast as those engines would go.

The moment that 707 lifted off the runway, every soldier on that airplane let out a rebel yell that would have made Stonewall Jackson proud. Finally we felt secure enough to breathe a sigh of relief that we had all beaten the Grim Reaper during our year in Vietnam.

It did not matter to anyone on that plane that we faced a long flight back to McChord Air Force Base at Seattle, Washington.

Flying from Vietnam to the West Coast of the USA involves passing the International Date Line which creates a weird phenomenon. Whatever date and time you leave Vietnam, you arrive back in the states at the same date and time. This takes a little getting used to.

We landed at McChord Air Force Base at Seattle and it was just a short distance to the civilian airport. The personnel there at McChord were quite accommodating and processed us through as quickly as possible.

I got over to the civilian airport and just walked down the line of airline counters shouting out, "Orlando, Orlando, Orlando, who has a plane going to Orlando?" I was in a frame of mind not to care what anybody thought. I guess everyone there cut me a little slack because I was in uniform and soon someone behind one of those counters raised their hand and said, "We have a flight just for you."

I bought my ticket and had just enough time to call my poor widowed mother back in Ocala, Florida and give her my flight information so she could meet me at the airport in Orlando, which was about 80 miles away from Ocala.

They gave me a first-class seat which I thought was awfully nice, although I really didn't get to enjoy it very much. I had been on the move for the last 24 hours and my seat mate on the flight home bought me a bottle of champagne to celebrate. After a few glasses of that bubbly beverage I slept until we landed at St. Louis. To this day I am grateful to that generous person who helped me celebrate my trip home.

The plane finally landed at the airport in Orlando and I was met by my widowed mother, and younger brother and sister. It proved to be a joyous occasion for all, especially for my mother.

I never really appreciated the strain my mother had had to bear with me being in Vietnam, until 30 plus years later when my son entered the Army and was sent off to fight in Iraq and Afghanistan. The pressure was incredible and I just about worried myself to death the whole time he was in harm's way over in the Middle East. My mother was a strong person and never let on how distressed she was about her elder son running around Vietnam on a lark, never thinking of the worry and concern he was causing her.

We all loaded up in the car and made the final leg of a journey home that had taken me halfway around the world. It was so good to get home and sleep in my own bed and relax during the 30 day paid leave the Army had graciously provided me.

My next duty station was to be Fort Lee, Virginia. Before I went to Vietnam, a year seemed like an eternity so I sold my faithful Pontiac Tempest before I left.

Upon my return, one of the first things I did (after paying off the mortgage on my widowed mother's house) was to buy an Oldsmobile 442. It was a high-powered machine that took me up to Fort Lee. After discovering the 44 deuce would not run in cold weather, I immediately traded it for a more sensible Oldsmobile Delta Royale.

Lt. Payne at LZ Baldy

CPT Payne, Headquarters Company Commander

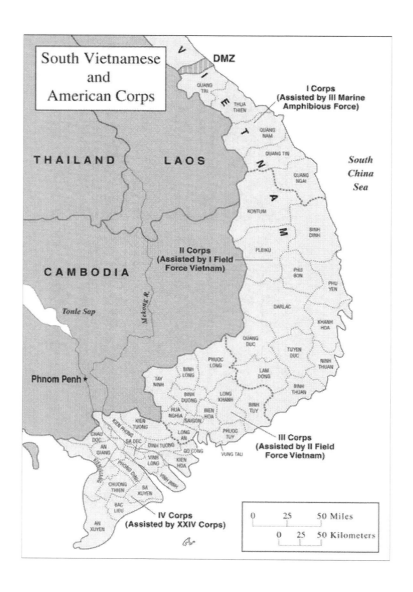

South Vietnamese and American Corps

DMZ

I Corps
(Assisted by III Marine
Amphibious Force)

THAILAND

LAOS

South
China
Sea

QUANG
TRI

THUA
THIEN

QUANG
NAM

QUANG TIN

QUANG
NGAI

KONTUM

BINH
DINH

II Corps
(Assisted by I Field
Force Vietnam)

PLEIKU

CAMBODIA

PHU
BON

PHU
YEN

Tonle Sap

DARLAC

KHANH
HOA

QUANG
DUC

TUYEN
DUC

NINH
THUAN

Phnom Penh ★

PHUOC
LONG

LAM
DONG

TAY
NINH

BINH
LONG

BINH
DUONG

LONG
KHANH

BINH
THUAN

HUA
NGHIA

BIEN
HOA

BINH
TUY

KIEN
TUONG

SAIGON

LONG
AN

PHUOC
TUY

III Corps
(Assisted by II Field
Force Vietnam)

CHAU
DOC

KIEN PHONG

SA DEC

DINH TUONG

GO CONG

AN
GIANG

VINH
LONG

KIEN
HOA

VUNG TAU

CHUONG
THIEN

BA
XUYEN

VINH BINH

BAC
LIEU

IV Corps
(Assisted by XXIV Corps)

AN
XUYEN

| 0 | 25 | 50 Miles |
| 0 | 25 | 50 Kilometers |

12 – Miracles and the Secret of Life

My second tour in Vietnam was was one of the highlights of my life. I had the privilege of flying Cobra gunships in an aerial rocket artillery unit of the 101st Airborne Division. My path to the backseat of a Cobra gunship was filled with many obstacles. I believe it is beneficial to describe that path because it could provide inspiration for others who are encountering obstacles in their own pathways of life.

From my early childhood I had always wanted to be a pilot. It didn't matter what type of aircraft; I just wanted to fly. As I got closer to the decision time in my late teens, I got the feeling I should go for Army aircraft rather than the jet fighters like my uncle had flown in the Air Force.

That intuition came as a result of eye exams I had taken in high school as I was preparing to go to college. Growing up I had always enjoyed good vision but apparently studying hard on the books weakened my vision a degree or two.

But not to be dismayed or discouraged, I still intended to become an Army aviator one way or the other. I went to the University of Florida and enrolled in the ROTC program. My first official Army physical examination occurred when I entered the Advanced ROTC program in my junior year.

I always indicated that I intended to volunteer for the aviation program, so I always was given the flight school vision test. And guess what? Every time I failed to meet the 20/20 vision requirement. Each failure only intensified my desire to become an Army aviator.

I even went to civilian optometrists to confirm the findings of the military medical examiners and to also look for ways to improve my vision. It was discouraging when the optometrists informed me that vision was a perishable commodity in that once it starts deteriorating, it never gets better. But I explained to the gentlemen it would have to get better because I was going to become an Army aviator.

As I got closer to graduation and pinning on my second lieutenants bars, I had to complete several more physical examinations and each time I volunteered for the flight school portion of the examination. And each time I failed. At one time my vision test results got up to 20-40 in one eye, which at that time still precluded entry into flight school.

For some reason all these eye exam failures did not destroy my inner vision of becoming an Army aviator. But at times it was a little discouraging.

I entered the Army as a second lieutenant and completed the Infantry Officers Basic Course and Jump School at Fort Benning, Georgia. And then I realized a dream I had had for several years. As a junior high school student I read a book by Ross G. Carter titled Devils in Baggy Pants. It was the story of a man who was a member of one of the first airborne units in the Army: the 504th Infantry Regiment (Airborne) of the 82nd Airborne Division.

It was a remarkable story of a soldier who not only went through the initial development of military airborne units, but also fought in every battle the 82nd Airborne Division participated in during World War II. He went from storming the beaches of North Africa, through Sicily, Italy, jumping into France on D-Day, and fighting across France and Germany until the end of the war. Immediately after the end of the war he served in America's guard of honor in Berlin.

It was a tragic irony that Carter died of cancer within a year of the war's end. His descriptions of his experiences with the 82nd Airborne Division not only inspired me to strive to become a member of that storied unit but he also said something in his book that had a life-changing effect on me.

He was once asked how he brought himself to jump out of an aircraft in the face of incredible perils. He simply answered that he never allowed the thought of being killed in battle to enter into his mind because down that road lay cowardice.

That one remark made me realize that we control our lives by how we think. Ross G. Carter was able to make himself jump into deadly situations by not allowing a certain thought to enter his mind.

I did not realize at the time that I was subconsciously following his example by not allowing the thought to enter my mind that I would fail to become an Army aviator. Sounds far-fetched but I will soon prove to you it is quite true.

After I had spent about a year with the 82nd Airborne Division at Fort Bragg, North Carolina, the Army decided my services were needed in Vietnam. So they sent me to one more school at Fort Lee, Virginia to learn how to be an Army supply officer, and then dispatched me to Vietnam where I was assigned to the 4th Infantry Division.

In earlier chapters I have recounted some of my adventures and misadventures with the 4th Division. It became apparent to me some Army procedures and regulations were only loosely followed in Vietnam, so I figured maybe this would be my opportunity to slip in under the radar and somehow pass the vision examination for flight school at the end of my first tour in Vietnam.

I was unaware I had been practicing mind games with myself ever since I began to fail flight school vision tests in college. The game was, every day I would mentally push myself like a weightlifter jerking 500 pound barbells. I would lift the mental barbells by thinking over and over that I wanted to be a pilot more than anything else and I was going to be a pilot. Sometimes I would actually strain myself from thinking so hard that I wanted to be an aviator.

As my first tour was coming to an end I decided to make my move. I began to frequent the military hospital up in Pleiku and develop relations with the optometry department. I figured if nothing else, I would bribe the doctor to obtain a passing vision test result. At this point I was desperate enough to resort to almost any measures to obtain my goal.

I scheduled another eye examination for my perpetual application to flight school and on that fateful day proceeded up to the eye clinic at Pleiku. I was very nervous because I knew one way or the other I was going to come away with an approved vision examination, and I hoped I would not do anything rash in the process because I knew it was going to happen. Much was riding on this exam.

I sat down in the chair and looked into one of those elaborate devices optometrists use to determine the vision capabilities of a person. You all know the drill; the examiner tells you to read a line of letters. He asked me and I read the line; he asked me to read another line, then the next. I read that line perfectly and then the next line down and the next.

I was beginning to wonder when he was going to get to the line I could never read before. But each line I again read with no problem.

Then he said something I had never heard before. He said to me, "You have perfect vision, don't you?" I paused for a moment to get over the shock of what he said and then quickly blurted out, "YES I DO!"

I began to hear Jimmy Swaggart saying Glory, Glory, Hallelujah over and over in my mind. Quickly I reconfirmed with the examiner his findings and asked him to confirm again to be doubly sure. He did and entered in the form that I had 20-15 vision.

To this day I have no explanation for the dramatic improvement in my vision other than a gift of God. In addition to mentally straining every day with the wish to become an aviator, I did throw in a few prayers here and there, so what can you say?

This event was a joyous occasion for me because I had overcome one of the main stumbling blocks keeping me out of flight school. Unfortunately, to my dismay I discovered there were more obstacles to come in my path to the backseat of a Cobra gunship.

Silly me, in my happiness of finally passing a flight school eye exam, I figured I would just submit my application and go straight to flight school at the end of my first tour in Vietnam. But you probably already guessed - something came up.

Before I left Vietnam after my first tour word came from the Pentagon my application was refused because officers in the Quartermaster Corps were not allowed to become pilots. As you remember, earlier I recounted how I accepted a Regular Army Commission in the Quartermaster Corps without knowing what it was. My acceptance was influenced by the wizened old sergeant major in the ROTC department at the University of Florida.

Instead of going to flight school, the Army sent me back to Fort Lee, Virginia where I became a company commander of one of the training companies in the Quartermaster School.

This branch situation was only a minor hangup compared to what I had had to overcome in passing the vision test. The solution was simple; just change branches. I immediately requested a branch transfer to the Transportation Corps because that branch was acceptable for flight training. I didn't really care at the time which branch it was, as long as they allowed their officers to enroll in flight training.

Now you don't think it was going to be that easy, do you? Well, you are right; it was not that easy, because the Transportation Corps refused to accept me. Something about a few questionable entries on my officer efficiency reports from my time with the 82nd Airborne Division and the 4th Infantry Division. It seems my habit of only following orders I felt like obeying had caught up with me.

Normally this turn of events would be a discouragement to a hopeful budding aviator, but not me. Somehow I knew something was going to happen that would open the door to flight school for me.

After about six months of hard yearning, lightning struck. I was sitting in my office reading the Army Times and suddenly a headline jumped off the page and hit me in the face like a bucket of cold water.

The headline read, "Army needs more pilots and flight training is now open to all branches." I was both overjoyed with adulation and at the same time totally confident it was going to happen. The only question I had ever had in my mind was how it would come about.

It came in the form of that headline announcing a need for more pilots and I was happy to be of service.

Again, my life had been greatly altered by the Vietnam War. The first time it prevented me from being thrown out of the Army for poor performance in the 82nd Airborne Division, and the second time it allowed me entrance into the U.S. Army flight school. I had to be leading a charmed life. My guardian angel Gabriel came through again.

An application for flight school consists of a one inch thick stack of paperwork that generally requires months of painstaking administrative detail work and physical exams but luckily I already had a complete application package ready to go.

I immediately shot it up to the personnel department and the Pentagon, and very shortly I received those coveted orders sending me to Primary Flight Training School at Fort Wolters, Texas. You would have had to look far and wide to find a happier person that day. I had to be the happiest person in America.

I was about to embark on a lifetime aspiration that would bring incredible adventures I would remember forever.

A happy Mack Payne in a TH-55 Trainer Helicopter at Fort Wolters, Texas

13 – Flight School - Fort Wolters

In 1969, Army rotary wing flight training consisted of two five-month phases. Phase 1 was primary training conducted at Fort Wolters, Texas, which was located about 40 miles west of Fort Worth, Texas. Phase 2 was conducted at the Army Aviation Headquarters and School at Fort Rucker, Alabama. There were some slight variations to the schedule but at that time the vast majority of students went through that program scenario.

I was looking forward to going to Fort Wolters because it was in Texas and I had never been to that great state. Being a bachelor at the time I found it is very easy to move. You merely loaded up all your personal stuff in the back of your Oldsmobile Delta Royale and boogied.

They say people associate memorable things with notable times in their lives. It is very interesting that the song Israelites by Desmond Dekker was popular at the time and played frequently on the radio. To this day when I hear that song it brings back fond memories of my departure from Fort Lee, Virginia and my journey out to Fort Wolters, Texas.

Of course on my way out to Texas I swung down through Florida to visit my widowed mother and then headed west after first stopping off to visit relatives in Dale County, Alabama.

It was very exciting when I hit the Texas state line. I was expecting to see Roy Rogers, Gene Autry, or John Wayne gallop by on their horses any minute. I was alarmed by the weather report. It was the first of July and I tuned in to a Dallas radio station and heard the high temperature that day was going to be 115°.

To a Floridian who could barely survive when the mercury hit 100° in Marion County, the thought of 115° seemed like sure death for everyone from heat strokes. I just knew everybody in Texas was going to die. But that's when I discovered what they mean when they say, "oh don's worry, it's a dry heat." And believe it or not, it was not that bad. You could actually exist in 115° temperatures out west.

I was to learn many things about the Lone Star State in the coming days. One interesting thing I heard on that same Dallas radio station was in Texas at that time, it was legal to kill an unfaithful wife and the person who participated with her in the affair. I found that to be a most interesting sociological phenomenon.

Another thing I immediately noticed about Texas was the road system. I think it put every other state's to shame. Not only did they have great interstate highways, most of those interstates had parallel dual-lane highways on either side for additional traffic. Also, most all of their farm-to-market two-lane roads had paved shoulders on either side that could accommodate a vehicle so another vehicle could safely pass in the normal lane.

It was customary for drivers on those roads to pull over and drive on the paved shoulders if a faster vehicle approached from the rear, making it unnecessary to pass in the oncoming lane. I was amazed that a state would and could build such a highway system.

I proceeded on west heading for Fort Wolters and passed through Dallas and Fort Worth, and as I passed through Dallas all I could say over and over was good night nurse and che-che bug, holy guacamole and I don't believe it! Dallas, Texas was and still is a go-go town. Many happy evenings were spent their by yours truly and friends during flight school.

Finally I arrived at Fort Wolters, conveniently located adjacent to the small Texas town of Mineral Wells. And yes they did have signs on the main street asking folks not to spit on the sidewalk.

I signed in at the school orderly room and was informed there was no room for student officers on post, and the local economy was currently swamped with the influx of flight school students.

I was told the only likely accommodations would be in one of the many trailer parks that had mushroomed up to serve the increase in population caused by the expansion of Fort Wolters. I do not stay in mobile homes, so I checked into the Cactus Motel and remained there for the duration of the training at Fort Wolters. Some of my fellow students thought it was funny that I lived in a motel but it did not bother me at all. The room service was great.

Our first day of flight school at Fort Wolters included all the usual ceremonies associated with the start of a new course of military training. Keeping in mind all the students there were on orders for Vietnam after flight school, I was a little surprised that the main emphasis of the school commander and others at the welcoming ceremonies was not about the dangers we were going to face in Vietnam. Their primary concern was in issuing dire warnings against any contact with the wives of Warrant Officer Candidates.

Going through flight training as an officer was like going to Club Med compared to the ordeal Warrant Officer candidates had to endure. According to military policy all aviators must be either commissioned or warrant officers. To become Army Aviators, enlisted men had to complete the Warrant Officer Candidate Program that ran concurrent with flight training.

They were referred to as WOC's and it was the apparent policy to make their lives hell. In addition to the flight training they were required to endure a strict officer training regimen that required living in and maintaining barracks. They were allowed infrequent weekend outings and it seemed like every one of them had a wife living in the local area.

It was obvious from the welcoming address of the school hierarchy there had been serious problems in the past with officer students taking advantage of WOC wives who were lonely and starved for attention. The whole situation appeared to be a little ridiculous. The primary concern of our school masters was not the lethal combat environment we were about to face but rather the moral turpitude of student officers being unleashed on wives of the WOCs.

The term "died and gone to heaven" was a perfect description of life as a student officer in P1 (Primary) flight training at Fort Wolters. The advantages are almost too numerous to mention but I will relate a few.

I always say that flight school was one of the best kept secrets in the Army. We only trained four hours per day, which left lots of time for the golf course and other assorted leisure activities. This schedule really beat the 18 hour days I endured while assigned to the 82nd Airborne Division. Not only did we have lots of idle time, we also had the money to pay for it. In addition to our regular generous pay we received flight pay and temporary duty pay since we were not permanently assigned to the flight school. That was another $750 in the paycheck every month, which in those days was a fair sum. Gas was only 30¢ per gallon and beer on tap was 25¢. Since I never developed a taste for beer, my preferred adult beverage was Canadian Club and the price for that was also correspondingly low.

The flight training schedule was an especially attractive feature. In the beginning there were two weeks of classroom training. We learned a few fundamentals of flying like what makes a helicopter go up or down and move backwards and forwards. A very valuable bit of information we also learned was the fundamentals of weather. We were taught how weather works, including why it gets cold and hot and other weather basics germane to flying, like what causes thunderstorms. Unlike a lot of Army training it was very practical and I still remember and use it to this day.

I learned something about psychology during those first two weeks of ground school. It was the procedure at flight school for the officer students to assemble at the student company headquarters and load onto buses for transportation to the particular training of the day.

During those first two weeks of ground school the buses would take us to the classrooms for training. The vast majority of students had no previous experience flying. All of us were a little concerned about the upcoming training, wondering if we would be able to successfully complete the course. That was true for all except for two students.

Every day as we were riding to and from the classrooms, both of these supposedly knowledgeable individuals would go on and on about how easy it is to fly a helicopter. They would say things like it was possible to train a monkey to fly a helicopter. All the other students including myself were a little dismayed by these two guys and we were thinking they would definitely be the best students because of their confident expressions of how easy it was to fly a helicopter.

As it turned out, both of these individuals washed out on the second day of training in the aircraft. According to the instructors both of them would freeze up when they touched the controls during flight. It was one of the most unusual displays of personality disorders I had ever seen.

It was explained to us they had such a morbid fear of flying they had to cover it up with braggadocious talk about how easy it is to fly. I thought they must really be screwed up to go through all the trouble involved with getting in the flight school when they were so afraid of flying. Obviously they did not encounter all the obstacles of getting into flight school that had gotten into my way, otherwise they would have given up sooner and not bothered us. I was glad to see them go because they were rapidly becoming pains in the butt.

After the completion of two weeks of ground school, our training schedule consisted of four hours of flight training per day, alternating each week between the mornings and afternoons. The kill-joys did stick in four hours of classroom training one day per week. That meant on four days of each week we only had four hours of training. The rest of the time was devoted to relaxation to recuperate from the rigors of flying those little helicopters.

Those two weeks of ground school were very helpful and informative but I could barely wait to begin the actual flight training. That first day of flight training finally came and I met my ace flight instructor. He was a civilian contractor named Mr. Avdeef who was a redheaded Egyptian with a striking resemblance to William Bendix. Our training was conducted with the TH-55 helicopter, which was a small little aircraft that would barely hold two adults and ran with the use of rubber bands (actually they appeared to be automotive fan belts). I couldn't have cared less because I was flying and it didn't matter what type of aircraft it was at that time.

I had no trouble picking up the flying techniques but I did have a few difficulties with my instructor. He had the habit of screaming at me in the intercom as I was trying to master the skill of flying. I assumed the instructors were told to behave that way toward students to weed out the ones that could not stand a little pressure. But if that was the case I had a little problem with the teaching philosophy.

Not to brag but I quickly mastered the art of flying those little trainer helicopters, yet Mr Avdeef continued to scream at me over the intercom. Finally one day during a post flight briefing I informed him he was my biggest obstacle in learning how to fly.

I cited this example: if you're trying to teach a two-year-old to walk, as they take their first step you don't scream in their face and slap them up beside the head. I told him his training techniques were much like that in that while I was trying to concentrate on the flying techniques he was constantly disturbing me.

He did not take my criticism lightly and was so incensed he gave me a failing grade for the next three training days. Three failures in a row are grounds for dismissal from the school but first they give you a check flight with an official Army instructor pilot. I welcomed the opportunity.

The next day after the third failure I was set up for a check flight with the big-time lead instructor pilot. I knew I could pass a check ride so I decided to have a little fun. What were they going to do? Send me to Vietnam?

Our training was conducted on little stage fields set up with six parallel mini-runways connected in the middle by a service road running perpendicular across the middle of all six runways. The runways were used for practice landings, takeoffs, and auto-rotations. For the uninitiated, auto-rotations are maneuvers used to land a helicopter safely after an engine failure.

Auto-rotations have to be done very carefully to avoid disastrous results. The reason they were practiced on short runways is because many times the helicopter would slide a short distance after an auto-rotational touchdown. A skilled pilot can set a helicopter down like a feather and land on a dime.

The examiner ended the check ride with the requirement to perform an auto-rotation. He selected one of the runways and instructed me to perform an auto-rotation and land at the cross driveway. I knew he meant for me to land on the runway as close to the cross drive as possible, knowing the aircraft might slide a little down the runway.

This is where I decided to have a little fun with the dude. I confirmed his instructions by saying, "You want me to land using runway 1 on the cross drive?" And he replied, "Yes." That's all I needed and proceeded to set the helicopter down like a feather on top of the cross drive next to runway 1. After we set down safely on the cross drive I looked over at him and asked if that was what he meant? He sat there for a moment agape then looked over at me and said simply, "Yes." I passed the check ride and Mr. Adveef was much nicer during the rest of my training in P1.

I had found in the military, if you know you are right you can stand up to people and it will work out to your benefit. I believe this little incident confirmed my belief. The key to this idea is ensuring you have the requisite amount of wisdom to know you are in the right (therein lies the challenge).

The primary purpose of P1 flight training was to teach the basics of flying and provide sufficient flight time for the aviator techniques to be absorbed by the students. That meant there was lots of just flying around gaining experience.

It did not take long to solo in those little helicopters and the event was celebrated by the ceremonial throwing of the new soloist into the Holiday Inn swimming pool. Once you soloed and demonstrated an ability to find your way back to the stage field, they allowed you to freely roam around and survey the North Texas terrain.

The school set up a navigation training program utilizing car tires painted white, and spread all over the area. The coordinates of each tire was recorded and we were given assignments to fly to designated tires.

Being a Florida Flatlander that area of Texas was mountainous to me, but the locals said it was only hilly. It was a lot of fun to fly in those areas because many of the tires would be placed at the tops of little hills and it was an adventure finding them, especially around an area called Possum Kingdom, which was a large, man-made lake and recreation area in the middle of some of those mini mountains.

It got a little old after a while flying to the same tire locations so there were some unnamed students who would fly down to a tire and pick it up with one of the skids on the helicopter and carry the tire to a new location, usually near swimming areas at Possum Kingdom Lake or popular rural eateries. It was always funny to see a little TH-55 helicopter flying by with a white tire hanging on one of the skids. To the best of my knowledge no one was ever caught in this activity.

The Bell Helicopter Company had a manufacturing plant in nearby Fort Worth and about midway through P1 our class was taken on a field trip to visit the plant to see how the helicopters we would soon be flying in Vietnam were built. It turned into a life-changing event for me.

You often hear the term "love at first sight." That is exactly what happened to me at the Bell helicopter plant when I first laid eyes on an AH-1G Cobra gunship. It was indeed love at first sight and I knew right then as I stood there staring at this incredibly beautiful aircraft that one day I would fly one of these sport cars of the air.

Up until that point I had not given much thought to what type of aircraft I would be flying after flight school. My main concern was successfully completing the school and I only gave passing thought to what I might be flying later. More than likely I assumed, it would be the ubiquitous Huey or maybe a big lumbering Chinook, or possibly even a Flying Crane. I had never considered the possibility of flying a Cobra gunship until that day on our field trip to the Bell helicopter plant. I was in love and I was hooked.

Little did I realize that my personal commitment to become a Cobra gunship pilot would present me with another series of challenges very similar to the battles I had had to fight just to get into flight school. More on that will come in the next chapter, so hold onto your hats, you are going to be thrilled at how I pulled off that cool accomplishment.

Speaking of leisure activities, I stumbled into one of those super serendipity situations at Fort Wolters. Early on I met a fellow student who hailed from San Antonio. He and his wife were temporarily without transportation and both were anxious to visit their families in San Antonio. They asked me if I would be interested in taking a trip down South in my new Oldsmobile Delta Royale automobile. They assured me if I would take them to San Antonio they would show me good time. No truer words were ever spoken.

Frank and Jan Ramert became great friends. Both their parents welcomed me with open arms. Frank's father was a retired Marine and Jan's father was a World War II Army Veteran who had done very well as a business owner in San Antonio. Both were very supportive of Frank and me in our training to fight in Vietnam and were determined to make us as happy as possible. They were all wonderful people.

We burned up US 281 every weekend going from Mineral Wells to San Antonio. Earlier I mentioned that Dallas was a happening place but San Antonio runs a close second. Thanks the parents we were wined, dined and entertained to the max. The entertainment was not restricted to just San Antonio. Some of it extended up to the Dallas area. We were treated to three exciting preseason football games where we watched the Dallas Cowboys led by Tom Landry play the Baltimore Colts, Green Bay Packers, and New York Jets.

It was a wonderful time and a great way to get my mind off the worries of Vietnam, even though I was not really much concerned. I had already been there and looked forward to going back as a pilot. I could easily accept the sympathic actions of well wishers.

Sadly, all good things must come to an end and we finished our P1 training in November of 1969. Our training at Fort Wolters concluded with a mass cross-country flight with the entire class dead-reckoning down to Seguin, Texas. It was a real spectacle for all those little helicopters to be flying so far on dead-reckoning, especially since about the only cross-country flying we had done before was searching for white tires around Possum Kingdom Lake.

That cross-country flight was even more difficult because they spread everybody out to make sure we could make it on our own without following someone. Luckily the previously mentioned Texas road system made navigation quite easy and all the little birds made it there and back without incident. Essentially all you had to do was follow I-35 south. We all made the trip safely and graduated from P1.

I have to brag here a little and let you know I graduated at the top of my class, which paid off with a few dividends in my up-coming flight training at Fort Rucker, Alabama.

With a little sadness I turned in my equipment, loaded my stuff into my Oldsmobile Delta Royale, checked out of the Cactus Motel, and headed for Alabama.

14 - Flight School - Fort Rucker

Fort Rucker, Alabama is situated down in the southeastern corner of the state. It is bordered by Ozark to the northeast, Enterprise to the southwest, and Daleville on the south side of the reservation near the main gate. I always figured there must be some powerful politicians in that area because Fort Rucker is the headquarters for all Army Aviation including training, and it keeps growing. It is The University of Rotary Wing Flight Training.

Going to Fort Rucker, Alabama had a little extra significance for me. I was born and raised in Florida, however both my parents were from Ozark. During my formative years our family would return to the old home places in Alabama at least two and sometimes up to six times per year.

There were lots of Payne and Snell relatives including grandparents, aunts, uncles, and cousins living in the small communities of Skipperville and Asbury just north of Ozark. I always loved to go up there because they all lived on farms out in the country and we always had fun with our relatives. We fished in my Grandfather Payne's numerous fish ponds, and hunted squirrels and dove. Sometimes if I could get away with it I would drive some of the farm tractors.

My grandfather's brother owned a classic old general store in downtown Skipperville and it was always an adventure to explore. My Grandfather Snell had a Norman Rockwell grandparent's home. It had a big front porch with a double swing we always loved to sit on and wave at the occasional car passing by. It seems everyone in rural Dale County waved at passing cars. In the back yard was a storybook barn with stalls, a hay loft, and all the other things that made it an exciting adventure to explore. Behind the barn and down the hill in the woods was a stream they had dammed up and it formed a perfect swimming hole where we spent many happy hours.

I looked forward to getting to Fort Rucker because of my fond memories of our family visits to Alabama. But those were only for short durations of a few days at the most. When I signed in to Fort Rucker for flight school it meant a stay of five months in the Wire Grass Region and it would change a few of my opinions.

This time things were a little different. Living in an area for five months is different from visiting for a few days. I had to settle into the south Alabama culture and society and it became apparent to me that even though all my forebearers came from that area, growing up in Central Florida gave me a different perspective on life.

Fort Rucker was a larger and more permanent installation than Fort Wolters, so I was able to secure an apartment in a fairly nice area rather than having to camp out in a motel. I was a little dismayed to discover that the only source of heat in this fairly nice apartment near the main gate of Fort Rucker, was a portable electric heater. My training there was from November until March and that year they experienced a particularly cold and rainy winter. Little did I know what all my Alabama relatives had to live through during those cold winters, while I was enjoying the fine weather of Central Florida where I grew up.

There were several other local sociological phenomena that bothered me slightly but nothing could really disturb the flight school high I was on which kept me happy all the time.

All my fellow students made it safely from Fort Wolters to Fort Rucker and we were soon hard at it on Phase II of our flight training. We discovered right away that flight training at Fort Rucker was not going to be the leisure "Club Med" type experience we had at Fort Wolters. There would be no more trips down to San Antonio with nights out at places like the Magic Time Machine Restaurant, Karams Tortilla Factory, or Little Hipps Bubble Room.

This phase of training was going to be serious business as we got closer to the reality of flying in combat. Not only was training fully scheduled every day, it was often conducted at night and on weekends. The rotten weather we experienced that winter contributed to longer training times. Many times we would sit in the ready rooms for hours and days waiting on good flying weather.

The first phase of training at Fort Rucker was the challenging instrument training conducted in the old reliable OH-13 helicopters. You've probably seen them many times in movies with their large, plastic bubble-covered cockpit and open frame tail boom.

These clunky ancient aircraft were a handful to fly compared to the agile little TH-55's to which we were accustomed. To make it even more difficult, all our training in the OH-13's was conducted under the hood. That means the only thing we could see as we were flying was the instrument panel. This created a challenging situation because not only was it difficult to learn flying on instruments, we also had to master blind-flying the unwieldy OH-13 at the same time.

We were anxious to complete the instrument training phase because that is when we would be allowed to fly the glorious and ubiquitous Huey helicopter. Everyone in our class would look with envy on the classes ahead because they were finished with instrument training and were flying Hueys, while we were still training in the old clunkers under the hood.

I mentioned earlier I had graduated at the top of our P1 class at Fort Wolters. That meant I became a candidate to receive a Standard Instrument Card (or in civilian terms, a license). This would fully qualify you to fly in instrument flying conditions or rather very foggy or cloudy weather where the visibility was limited. Of course I would have the privilege of enduring extra training in the Instrument Flying Phase while my lesser skilled classmates went on to Huey training. The vast majority of Army Rotary Wing Pilots at that time were issued Tactical Instrument Cards, meaning they only received a minimum of instrument training that barely introduced them to the challenging skill of flying Instrument Flight Rules.

On one hand it was nice to be recognized as a top graduate of P1 and be a recipient of a Standard Instrument Card, but it meant a few extra days of training in the clunky OH-13's under the hood. I was a little envious of my lesser ranked classmates who were able to move ahead to training in the exciting Hueys.

This also meant I had the opportunity to endure more time in the link trainer. Link trainers are little movable boxes configured like the inside of a cockpit. Trainees go inside the little box, or link, close it up, and operate the controls and instruments as if in a real aircraft. The link would move in response to control movements, so the student inside would get the sensation of actually flying an aircraft as the link responded to the student input.

Each link trainer was monitored by an instructor. The room where the link trainers were situated was very large and had dozens and dozens of link trainers set up with an instructor's desk adjacent to each one. When I went through the program all the instructors were civilian females employed by a contractor. This presented more opportunities to stir up trouble and I immediately took advantage of the opening.

My instructorette, Mrs. Tew, was a cheeky little blonde lady who made it too easy for me to have a little fun. During a lull in our link training sessions we were chatting and I commented about all the women working in the room. Knowing this would upset her, I stated it was my belief that a woman's place was in the home. It was obvious she did not agree with that statement. As she got more upset I innocently continued to press the issue defending my opinion until she lost her composure.

I'm sure you have already guessed what happened. Despite the fact I had been receiving top grades in the link trainer, after that conversation I received three red failing grades in a row which led to another check out by a supervisor. Of course I passed the check flight with flying colors but for the rest of the link training phase my relations with Mrs. Tew were very cool. She no longer bored me with her mindless chatter.

Finally I successfully completed the instrument course and was the happy recipient of a Standard Instrument Card, which at the time was a nice little thing to brag about. Later it came in very handy and there's no doubt in my mind on more than one occasion it saved my life and several others, so it was worth the extra effort.

Finally, it was on to training in Hueys. This part of our training was divided into two phases. The first was dedicated to transition training where we learned the basics of the Huey helicopter and how to fly and maintain the aircraft. The second phase and to me the most interesting, was tactical training where we learned the specific techniques that we would be required to know when flying for real in Vietnam.

In addition to learning the basics of flying, I also learned some very valuable lessons about leadership. Those lessons I learned applied not only to military leadership techniques but to any supervisory subordinate situation in or out of the military.

Each class section was organized with a section commander who was a captain, and about 20 to 25 instructor pilots. Each of the instructor pilots would have two student pilots assigned to them for training. Unlike our previous training where the instructors were civilian contractors, all the instructors in this phase of our training were Vietnam combat veterans. They were generally the best pilots and were carefully selected to train new pilots.

In our Huey training at Fort Rucker we had one set of instructors for the transition training and another set for the tactical training. It was interesting to note that despite the fact they were good aviators, the attitude of the instructors in the transition phase was very poor, and I attributed it to the behavior of the section commander.

I cannot put my finger on it other than merely saying he had a bad attitude. He displayed an unspoken indication he was not happy with his job and would prefer to be someplace else. It showed in his behavior as the leader of training. It was especially noticeable when the instructors would sit around, and spent a minimum amount of time talking about flying and a maximum of time talking about unrelated subjects.

The instructors in our tactical training were totally different. The officer in charge was all business and he insisted his instructors maintain the same attitude. The difference in the professionalism of this group was like night and day when compared to our instructors in the transition phase.

This was one of the most obvious displays of good versus bad leadership I had ever seen. It was amazing how much of a tangible difference the leader of a group can make on how the group performs. I always considered that learning experience to be as valuable as our flight training.

During this phase of our flight training we also had a few administrative matters to deal with, including making our requests for additional training in other types of aircraft after the basic flight school.

If you remember in the last chapter I described how it was love at first sight with me and the Cobra gunship. Unfortunately I discovered it was much easier to have the desire to be a Cobra pilot than to actually become one. Silly me, I figured all a person had to do was put in a request for the course and it would be accepted, especially for someone at the top of his class. But as you may have surmised, it wasn't going to be that easy.

My first application was refused with the excuse that Quartermaster Officers did not attend the Cobra Transition Course because Quartermaster officers do not serve in Cobra gunship flying positions.

Naturally I disagreed with that reasoning. The way I looked at it, the Army needed Cobra pilots and as long as they were ready, willing, and able to fly the aircraft, branch designation was irrelevant. As usual, I found the higher-ups did not share that opinion. There is more to come on this later.

Our training at Fort Rucker came hot and heavy and I had very little time to enjoy my unheated apartment in Daleville.

The first phase of our Huey training consisted of much practice in the basics. The training fields at Fort Rucker were laid out similar to those at Fort Wolters, with six short, parallel runways. They were used to practice takeoffs, landings and auto-rotations. Auto-rotations in Hueys were more challenging than those in the diminutive TH-55's. The Hueys were much larger and heavier, and far less forgiving.

When a Huey turns over on its side and the main blade is still turning, it has a tendency to rip the transmission out, and this can be very hazardous to the health of the crew. I discovered if you concentrated on your technique you could set a Huey down as soft as a feather, just like TH-55.

The transition training was very good and we all became competent Huey pilots, which paved the way for our next phase of training. I assumed since this was the last we would receive before going to Vietnam, only the best and brightest instructors would be utilized in this final training phase.

It was here we learned all the intricacies of formation flying, and landing and taking off from confined areas. About the only thing missing that would have made this training more realistic would have been bullets flying through the canopy.

The instructors in this phase were very helpful because they all had lots of interesting war stories to tell us. Some were even a little hair-raising and we could probably have done without those because it raised our levels of concern.

With the exception of the two students who washed out in our first week of flight training back at Fort Wolters, the entire class successfully completed flight school, despite the challenging maneuver we had to preform at the end of our training.

It was a tradition at Fort Rucker for each graduating class to preform a mass fly-by. That is a maneuver where the entire class assembles in a tight formation of more than one hundred helicopters lined up in three rows side-by-side, and flies over a reviewing stand where all the school brass and student friends and relatives can view the results of our training.

My class graduated at the end of March, 1970, and you know the old saying that March either comes in or goes out like a lion. That old saying held true for our class because that March definitely went out like a lion with high winds. It was difficult to fly an aircraft alone on a windy day, so trying to maintain a tight formation of over 100 helicopters flown by student aviators in windy conditions was a challenging experience.

I was glad to be flying in one of the outer rows, which would have made a quick exit from the formation easy if it all fell apart, but unfortunately the aircraft flying on the inner row next to mine was piloted by one of the weaker students and he was having difficulty maintaining his position. Keeping in mind the aircraft were only one rotor wing apart, if everyone did not hold their correct positions there could have been a big catastrophe in front of all the dignitaries and families.

The erratic pilot caused me more than a little concern. I hate to say much about that pilot because he later became a medevac pilot in the 101st Airborne Division and performed many heroic rescue missions before he was wounded in a crash and medevaced back to the States.

We successfully completed the final requirement and we landed our aircraft and were bused back to the reviewing field and received our official U.S. Army

Aviator Wings - a happy day. Next stop for most of us was Vietnam.

The vast majority of students from our class did head straight for Vietnam, but a few were sent to transition courses first.

Earlier I mentioned I had my heart set on becoming a Cobra gunship pilot and my initial application was rejected. I did not let this little setback discourage me. Again, I knew that one way or another I was going realize my dream of being a Cobra gunship pilot.

During my Fort Rucker flight training I continued to submit applications for Cobra school and they continued to be rejected. I even called the Department of the Army Personnel Office at the Pentagon on several occasions pleading my case, but to no avail.

I was ordered to stop sending applications but did not stop me from sending requests. What were they going to do – send me to Vietnam? It even got to the point where I was threatened with a court-martial if I continued to apply. They did not realize how determined I was, so I didn't have any choice...I had to keep applying.

I ended up making 43 applications for Cobra school, all of which were rejected. Finally as my flight training was ending, I made one final application and I did not receive a response before graduation.

At the end of flight school new assignments were posted on the bulletin board. There were many graduates and as I moved down the list of names looking for mine, I was noticing where everyone was going and most were headed straight to Vietnam, with a few going to transition courses. I finally came to my name on the list wondering where I would be sent. I looked over and next to my name was the Cobra Transition Course at Hunter Army Airfield, Savannah, Georgia.

When I saw that, I was again one of the happiest people in America. I have no idea why I was approved for the Cobra Transition Course. The only thing I could figure was they either got tired of hearing from me or they figured anybody who wanted to fly Cobras that badly must be crazy, so they said, let him go for it.

With orders for Cobra school in hand, I loaded up my Oldsmobile Delta Royale and headed for Savannah, Georgia – the home of Hunter Army Airfield and the US Army Cobra School.

15 - Flight School – Hunter Army Airfield

It was only a short drive of 150 miles from Fort Rucker to Hunter Army Air Field in Savannah and when I signed in at the student officer orderly room I received a pleasant surprise.

My Cobra transition course began on 1 May and I signed in one month early. Normal policy had always been when an officer reported in prior to a class date they would be assigned some type of temporary duty to keep them busy.

Expecting the same here, I asked the clerk where I was to report on the next duty day and he responded, "The class starts on May 1." I asked again what I would be doing in the meantime and again he responded, "The class starts on May 1." One last time I asked where I should report the next day and for the third time he responded, "Your class starts on May 1." Three times was enough for me. I realized they did not want to see me until May 1 when my class started. I was granted an additional informal 30 day leave that year.

Unlike Fort Wolters and Fort Rucker, Hunter Army airfield was located near a large metropolitan area so there was no problem finding a place to stay or entertainment. During my 30 day hiatus from duty, there was plenty of time to investigate the many entertainment and dining facilities in the Savannah area. I became very familiar with many of the establishments along the revitalized riverfront district, including well-known restaurants like the Pirates House and Johnny Harris's restaurant. I was also able to make several trips down to visit my widowed mother in Florida.

Finally, the first of May came and I began the Cobra transition course. It was conducted at Hunter Army airfield and I was told it used to be a former Cold War B-52 air base. It still had bunkers where atomic bombs were stored while awaiting delivery by the B-52s.

Since all the students were already qualified aviators, the training was conducted much like a gentleman's course. The class had about 25 to 30 students that were paired up with an instructor. I was under a little pressure because my student partner was an aviation maintenance officer from nearby Fort Stewart, and I could tell he intimidated our instructor pilot with his mechanical knowledge. I am sure he knew more about the mechanics of a Cobra than the instructor pilot. Consequently the IP tended to ask me all the tough questions about the aircraft mechanics.

I had a tough time answering those questions about the mechanical aspects of a Cobra. The engine compartment appeared to me to be a can of worms so I had to overcome that deficiency with flying expertise.

I have to admit the experience of flying a Cobra gunship for the first time was an extremely exciting event. Every day we would take off from a Hunter Army airfield and fly over to the nearby Fort Stewart reservation where our flight training area was located. It was a joy to pull pitch (the in vougue term for lifting off the ground in a helicopter) every morning.

In the future in Vietnam when I became a truly experienced Cobra pilot, I realized the Cobra transition course had been merely a familiarization of the aircraft. The real training was done on the job in combat conditions. In those situations you learn fast or die.

It has been a while but if memory serves, if we fired any live rockets during the transition course, it was very few. I can imagine it must have been a very frightful experience for the IP's when student pilots fired live rockets, because it is an exacting art form that requires lots of practice to be done correctly.

I had one embarrassing moment during the transition course. In a Cobra, the pilot sits in the rear seat and it's very difficult to see forward because of the console that's directly in front, so a new pilot will have a tendency to raise the seat up as high as it will go to afford better vision.

One of the main points the instructors always stressed was when you raise the seat, make sure the release lever is firmly set. The travel distance of the seat was about six inches, which could result in the seat dropping that six inches back down if the release lever was not properly secured.

Unfortunately one day I did not insure that my seat release lever was firmly set. My instructor pilot decided to do one of his favorite training maneuvers - the dreaded auto-rotation. The instant he cut the engine and we began to fall like a rock, and my seat also fell like a rock. It shook him up so badly he actually raised his voice at me for the first time. He was a very polite young man and it was the first time he ever became visibly upset with me. I apologized profusely and promised not to do that again.

Flying a Cobra required much more attention to detail and technique than did flying the Huey. The Cobra was designed for one thing and one thing only, to deliver ordnance onto an opposing force. It had certain design features that required much more precise control applications. There were deadly consequences for the pilot who failed to apply such techniques.

The cord (width of a rotor blade) on a Huey is about 15 inches. On a Cobra the rotor blade cord is 31 inches, so it can move much more air than Huey blades. This puts a lot more stress on the rotor mast. A rough jerk on the collective, which controls the angle of the rotor, could easily rip the rotor off the mast. This would make continued flight of the aircraft impossible and bring about the imminent death of the pilots.

Another little interesting feature of the design of a Cobra gunship is that the vertical tail has a permanent cantilever, which means the pilot has to constantly monitor the trim of the aircraft in a dive. These and many other design aspects of the aircraft made it a challenge to fly. For those who mastered the art of flying a Cobra it was hard to be humble and not assume an air of superiority over their fellow helicopter pilots.

One of the most interesting aspects of flying the Cobra was was the steep dive maneuver. And when I say steep, I mean steep! We had practiced diving at fairly shallow angles and then one day the IP demonstrated steep diving, which meant flying straight down. This was a little disconcerting because rotary wing aircraft are not designed for that type of maneuver.

It was a little challenging to learn how to get comfortable flying a helicopter straight down toward the Earth, but that skill came in handy when we were flying over the Kingdom of Laos.

All good things must come to an end, and Cobra School ended too soon for me, as I was enjoying the cultural delights of Savannah. But there was a war going on and we had deadly business that needed to be taken care of over in the Orient.

My time at Hunter Army Airfield ended almost a year of flight training and I was ready to go put it to use in Vietnam.

16 – Back to the Future

The name for this chapter comes from a popular movie because it is an apt description of my situation as I began my second tour in Vietnam. I had been there before and was familiar with what was going on, yet I was about to begin a most fantastic new year in the same locale "rockin and sockin" the bad guys with Cobra gunship rockets.

As opposed to my first tour, this time the powers in charge sent me on the southern route departing from Oakland, California. I decided to go ahead and have a pre-Vietnam R&R by arriving in San Francisco to few days early to enjoy a nice stay at the Fairmont Hotel in the heart of the city. Keith Whittingslow, a fellow student in P1 and a native of California, recommended that particular hotel and it lived up to its billings.

I made friends with a taxi driver who at the end of my R&R in San Francisco, drove me over to the Oakland terminal to show his appreciation for my service to the country. Surprisingly, I found many patriots in that part of the country even though the area was well-known for its opposition to the Vietnam War. It was reassuring to know Clint Eastwood was born in San Francisco. Luckily for me, I never encountered any war protesters, going or coming.

Since this was my second visit to Vietnam, I was a little older and wiser than the last time, so it wasn't as scary and mysterious. This time it had more of a routine nature to it since I had done the drill before. One of the other benefits of my experience was this time I knew one year was not all that long.

For instance, before my last tour I sold a perfectly good Pontiac Le-Mans automobile thinking a year was an eternity and the car would fall apart before I got back. This time I parked my Oldsmobile Delta Royale in my widowed mother's garage with instructions to crank it up once per month. I was so happy I did because when I got home after my second tour, my car was sitting there like a faithful steed ready to go.

Utilizing the southern route to Vietnam demonstrated a very fascinating geological reality. Looking at a Mercator projection map of the Earth, it appears the southern route would be more direct and shorter than the northern route through Alaska and Japan. But on the contrary, the southern route is a little longer, making a lengthy, boring flight even more so. Despite that, the long flight was probably much better than spending several days on a troopship.

One benefit of the southern route was being able to see new and different places. We stopped off for a while in Hawaii and I found it to be very agreeable. I can understand why people like to go there.

We also stopped over for refueling at Wake Island, without a doubt, the most isolated, lonely, desolate place I had ever seen and I have no inclination ever to return.

On this trip my entry point into Vietnam was the massive complex way down south at Long Binh near Saigon, rather than the sunny, laid-back Cam Ranh Bay. Being a country boy from rural Central Florida, I preferred the latter entry point rather than Long Binh, with all its hustle and bustle. It had the unpleasant features of a big city people had put up as a trade-off between the good life of the rural areas and the economic opportunities found in a big city.

Long Binh was where all the big military headquarters were located. General Westmoreland hung his hat there when he was not flying around visiting and supervising troops. At the personnel processing unit I met a smooth-talking and impressive-looking young man who was processing out on his way home. While chatting he mentioned to me his job in Vietnam had been to conduct the daily briefings for General Westmoreland and his staff. I thought to myself, some people have all the luck. All you need is good looks and a great baritone voice to get the best jobs.

Also located at Long Binh was the main U.S. Army stockade where all the incorrigibles were sent. The stockade was referred to as LBJ, short for Long Binh Junction or Lyndon Baines Johnson, depending on the mood of the day.

One of the other differences between my two tours was on the first tour, the Army went through the formality of assigning personnel to a unit prior to deployment, which was often changed upon arrival in country. On the second tour they made no pretense of being so organized. I was assigned to USARV (United States Army Vietnam) as a Cobra gunship pilot; consequently, I had no idea where I might be sent in country.

Soon that question was answered. I received orders for the 101st Airborne Division located way up north at Camp Eagle near the old city of Hué. I was very pleased with this development and looked forward to serving in another airborne division besides the 82nd. Another desirable feature of this assignment was that I would go back up north, far away from the water-logged rice paddy country of the southern part of Vietnam.

Before I knew it I was aboard a C-130 heading north to Camp Eagle, home of the 101st Airborne Division with its gallant reputation of kicking the Germans' butts at Bastogne during World War II.

16 - The 101st Airborne Division

When I joined the 101st Airborne Division it was deployed at three locations. The southernmost brigade was located at Phu Bai, adjacent to the area's airport. Another brigade, along with the division headquarters, was located a few miles up Highway 1 at a facility known as Camp Eagle, which looked similar to a garbage dump from the air. Both of these installations were located south of the old city of Hue not far from the beautiful South China Sea. The third brigade was located a little further up the road at Camp Evans, about 20 miles north of the city.

Before I go forward with my 101st adventures, I would like to quickly describe to the reader how Cobra gunships were employed in an airmobile division like the 101st. There were three applications. One was the escort mission. The lift units had organic gunships (a permanent part of) assigned to them for the purpose of escort duties wherever their Hueys would be operating. This meant lots of flying time for escort gunship pilots because lift companies were always busy flying missions.

The second application was in the reconnaissance mode. The Division's cavalry squadron had Cobras assigned to support its small recon helicopters and its organic infantry units known as "Blues." Cobra pilots in this unit also racked up many flight hours in support of recon missions.

The third application was in support of the Division's artillery assets. In traditional Army divisions at the time, the artillery was organized in a brigade level organization to support three infantry brigades. In an airmobile division the Division Artillery Command was supplemented with a battalion of Cobra gunships. This gave the artillery forward observer in the field with his infantry unit additional firepower assets to call upon.

This was a very efficient system for requesting support because there were gunship assets available within the artillery communications system, which meant gunship support could arrive on station within minutes of being requested by the forward observer. This was important because many times precious minutes in fire support missions could have life or death consequences. This application was referred to as Aerial Rocket Artillery or in common Army parlance, ARA.

The two primary missions of ARA units were fire missions and landing zone preps. This resulted in ARA pilots accumulating fewer hours than their gunship pilot counterparts but their flight hours were much more action filled.

ARA gunships were literally "killing machines." They were not intended for time-consuming missions like escort or reconnaissance. Whenever ARA gunships launched on a mission, somebody was going to die.

Upon arrival at camp Eagle, I was assigned to the division's ARA Battalion which played out much to my satisfaction.

The designation for the ARA battalion assigned to the 101st was the 4th Battalion of the 77th Field Artillery. It consisted of three batteries and each battery had three flight platoons. Each flight platoon had two aircraft which meant on paper, the battalion could launch 18 rocket-shooting aircraft. The term "battery" is used in artillery units to designate company-sized units. Since the ARA battalion was assigned to an artillery command, it used artillery unit designations, so the company-sized units were referred to as batteries.

The normal weapons configuration for ARA gunships was four large rocket pods with a total capacity of 76 - 2.5 inch, folding fin, World War II vintage aerial rockets. These time-proven weapons could be fitted with a variety of warheads, including 10 and 17 pound high explosive, flechette (nails), CS gas, and anti-tank, to name a few. The gunships also had a chin turret normally outfitted with a minigun and a grenade launcher. Depending on the abilities of the battery maintenance personnel, on occasion the chin turret guns would actually work, but that was okay with me because the rockets were what really packed a punch in the battlefield arena.

A Cobra outfitted with four of the large 19 round rocket pods created a distinct appearance that was immediately recognizable, causing ARA gunships to become known as heavy hogs. That moniker sounded good to me because they could really lay down the steel on the target.

Initially I was assigned to B Battery at Camp Eagle where I got my introduction to combat flying. It was a good experience flying with B Battery because they had many outstanding pilots. But after just a few short weeks I was reassigned to A Battery over at Phu Bai.

As I mentioned earlier, Camp Eagle from the air looked very much like a garbage dump, which was actually a compliment. In a combat environment it is better for facilities to be arranged in a haphazard manner so as to make them more defensible and harder to hit in a wholesale manner. Camp Eagle was laid out in a very random fashion which made it very difficult for me to locate the B Battery landing pad from the air whenever I had the occasion to go there.

On the other hand, the airfield facilities over at Phu Bai were the exact opposite in their layout. The US Marines formerly operated in this northern area of Vietnam before they were relieved by Army units. The

Marines have a reputation for spit and polish and even in combat situations they appeared to apply that philosophy.

The Army aviation assets located at Phu Bai occupied former Marine quarters and they had constructed buildings very similar to those you might find on a military post back in the States. These carefully laid out and professionally built two-story structures were quite different from the humble shacks that housed the Army units over at Camp Eagle. I preferred the humble shacks to the nice wooden buildings of Phu Bai.

I had been assigned to B battery just long enough to get to know the pilots there and they were a bunch of wild and crazy guys capable of great feats of flying skill and heroic deeds. When I moved over to A Battery at Phu Bai I was not nearly as impressed with the personnel, with the exceptions of Big Jim Fadden, and Ronnie Pepper, along with J.C. Borom and the crazy maintenance officer Rick Scruggs, both of whom will be mentioned later.

I was told the reason for my reassignment to A Battery was that their commander was leaving in about a month and since I was a ranking Captain, they installed me as the battery executive officer. I assumed this was to provide a little continuity for the unit when the battery commanders changed.

Apparently I proved to be a good luck charm for A Battery. The week before my arrival an aircraft crashed on a night mission, killing both pilots. One week after my departure, an entire former flight platoon was killed during a night mission in the same vicinity as the accident that had occurred the year before. During my stay at A Battery we suffered only a few minor casualties and no deaths of any of our pilots.

The outgoing battery commander will remain nameless for several reasons. Number one, I was not overly impressed with his leadership abilities. In my opinion things appeared to be a little slack in the unit. Also, an incident relayed to me by Rick Scruggs later sealed the deal on my opinion of the outgoing commander.

Just about every one in Vietnam, including commanders, looked forward to the day when they would leave the country and return to the good old USA. The outgoing battery commander was no different. In the short time I was there with him he constantly talked about how happy he was going to be when he could go home to be with his loving wife. I assumed he must have a very loving relationship with her from both his comments and the pictures of her in his quarters.

Apparently he could not wait to reunite with his loving wife. According to Capt. Scruggs, the night before he was to depart, the battery commander and Capt. Scruggs decided to go over to the 85th Evac Hospital Officers Club to celebrate the occasion of his departure. The 85th Evac Officers Club was very popular with all the surrounding aviation units because there were lots of female medical personnel who frequented the club.

On this particular evening which was the eve of the outgoing commander's departure, he struck up a conversation with a nurse and soon the two disappeared. It came time to return to their quarters so Capt. Scruggs began to look for the commander. Upon inquiring of several individuals, it was determined the nurse and her new-found friend, the outgoing commander, had gone to her quarters. Capt. Scruggs went looking for the him to let him know it was time to go.

Much to his surprise he discovered the two actively engaged in he-ing and she-ing in the nurse's quarters. Needless to say the outgoing commander was very embarrassed by this little episode. The only thing I could assume was that his tour lasted one day too long and I just hope he did not take any unwanted gifts of an STD nature back to his wife. This was one of the reasons I did not have a favorable impression of A Battery.

In my job as the battery executive officer I did not get to do much flying, other than the occasional fill-in mission. The learning curve for becoming a proficient rocket shooter was steep and it required much of a one year tour to master the skill. I was very anxious to do as much flying as possible and could hardly wait for a flight position to open up.

Upon the departure of the battery commander I stepped in as the temporary commander, awaiting the arrival of the new commander. I had to host several IG inspections being conducted by the Battalion Headquarters shortly after I assumed my position. Unfortunately, much of the battery administration had not been properly executed in the past and the inspection results painfully revealed that fact. Capt. Scruggs commented after one inspection, "They did not even acknowledge we were an Army unit." In addition to being an excellent instructor pilot and maintenance officer, he was one of the funniest people I have ever known.

There was work to be done and paperwork was neither my forte nor preferred activity, but in the Army when assigned a job, you say "Yes sir!" and get to it, and that is what I did.

I did not need to worry too much about the direction of the battery because there was help on the way in the form of the new battery commander, Maj. Richard L. Mills. In an opinion not shared by all, I considered him to be one of the best officers I ever served under. He very efficiently straightened out the battery in a short period of time. Some of his methods were a little unorthodox but very effective in my estimation.

An example was once at a pilots meeting, he looked at everyone with his steely eyes and grimly stated the crew chiefs were not the pilots' "niggers." You could have heard a pin drop in the room. He was very peeved at the sloppy pilots leaving trash in the cockpits. After that statement all pilots were very careful to tidy up the cockpit after every mission.

I enjoyed working with Major Mills. He tirelessly addressed and corrected the deficiencies in the battery. The previous battery commander had been rather slack in his control of the pilots. The first thing Major Mills did upon his arrival was establish a pilots meeting every morning in the operations room.

This had an amazingly positive affect on the pilots despite their griping. In the past all they did was fly missions, sleep and go to the officers club. At first there was grumbling about having to actually get up every morning and attend a meeting, but it soon became evident that the daily briefings/meetings were having a positive effect on morale and discipline.

Major Mills used this type of positive leadership on all phases of battery operations. He did not hesitate to call a spade a spade. In one of those meetings he referred to the battery vehicle maintenance officer as the worst he had ever seen and the particular officer was present in the meeting. No one cracked a smile as an icy pall fell over the room.

Everyone quickly realized it was not a good idea to cross Major Mills. One time a young warrant officer who had just arrived at the battery asked the Major for the time, and he quickly and sternly replied to the young inquirer it was time for him to buy a watch. That was typical of Major Mills' no-nonsense method of communicating with his subordinates.

In addition to his leadership and administrative abilities he was also a proficient karate expert, which he demonstrated using the scrap lumber from our quarters remodeling job.

Luckily for me after a few months as the battery executive officer, a new Capt. was assigned who outranked me. This meant he would become the battery executive officer and I could finally realize my goal of becoming a flight platoon leader and fly missions everyday.

Mack Payne flying over Vietnam

A Battery Headquarters staff

WO Kimball, CPT Latham, Base Cmdr & CPT Payne

Major Mills, WO J.C. Borom and CPT Payne

Major Mills, CPT Payne, 1SG Jenkins

Heinz Guderian, military communications innovator

187

Mack Payne in front of wooden buildings at Phu Bai

Mack Payne refueling at Phu Bai (notice the strict adherence to the rules of always being armed and wearing Nomex flight suits)

Camp Eagle Entrance

18 - Big Jim Fadden

A book about my Vietnam flying memoirs would not be complete without a chapter devoted to my friend Jim Fadden. He was truly a larger than life individual who actually could bowl overhanded if he took a notion. He looked like a movie star, was good athlete, a super gunship pilot, and a natural leader.

I first met him when I was a sophomore at the University of Florida. He was an incoming freshman who swaggered in as a worldly graduate of the American High School in Heidelburg, Germany. His father was in the military so he had seen a lot more of the world than all the other Florida Flatlanders.

We both lived at the Cooperative Living Organization just off campus for three years. He was an amazing guy and was constantly followed around by a crowd of admirers. He had the Evel Knevel knack for always doing something interesting and adventuresome like enticing an inebriated classmate to climb the TV tower at Florida Field and then encouraging the climber to jump. It was suspected he was involved in secret missions like stealing the Confederate Battle Flag off the Kappa Alpha Fraternity House.

He displayed his natural leadership abilities at a CLO event where for some reason we had rented a U-Haul truck and gotten it hopelessly stuck in the mud. He quickly organized the group into a cohesive unit that successfully freed the vehicle from the mud in no time.

On one occasion I remember he calmed down an unruly drunken classmate merely by giving him the evil eye. Jim was a serious weight lifter and his physique could be very intimidating.

We both enrolled in the Army ROTC program and upon graduation went our separate ways, never realizing we would bump into each other four years later in the same Army unit in northern Vietnam, flying Cobra gunships. For me to be flying Cobras was the result of overcoming many obstacles, but for Jim Fadden it was something he was born to do.

When assigned to A Battery at Phu Bai, I was surprised to discover that a Captain Jim Fadden was one of the flight platoon leaders. I thought there was no way it could be that Jim Fadden but lo and behold, it was him in person.

Just as he did at the University of Florida, he always had a retinue of mooney-eyed admirers following him around. But he was in his element as an ARA flight platoon leader. His natural leadership abilities were on full display as he managed his pilots and missions.

He also had a keen sense of humor. Once he convinced one of his crew chiefs, who was normally a very well-mannered, low-keyed individual, to go to my quarters, wake me up and inform me of some dire news that required my immediate attention. This occurred at about 2:00 AM after Captain Fadden had gotten him all liquored up. The poor crew chief was so embarrassed he avoided me for weeks afterward. Of course Big Jim and his posse had a big laugh at my expense.

19 - Combat Flying in I Corps

During my time in country, South Vietnam was divided into four geographic areas for combat planning. These areas were designated as Corps, with I Corps in the North, and the southernmost being IV Corps. The 101st Airborne Division operated in the northern half of I Corps and its area of operation ran from just north of Danang up to the DMZ, and from the South China Sea to the Laotian border.

There were named fire bases spread throughout the division's area of operation. Some of the names were historically relevant like Nuts, Anzio, Berchtesgaden, Veghel, and Bastogne, which reflected on the division's

World War II heritage. Others were good macho military names like Rifle, Brick, Spear, Arrow, Razor, and Airborne. And of course there were a few with sentimental names like Nancy, Helen, Stella, and Jane, probably named after some staff officer's wife or girlfriend back home.

Knowledge of firebase locations was critical to the type of missions we flew. I was a little surprised I was never required to memorize the firebase locations because it was such an important thing for a pilot to know. All our missions were referenced by firebase locations and map coordinates. I assumed it all went back to the, "This is Vietnam, don't worry about it" attitude I noticed during my first tour.

I took it upon myself to commit the location of every firebase to memory. As a result I gained a reputation as a good navigator, until that dark day in the Kingdom of Laos where that hard-earned reputation took a big hit. This incident will be addressed later.

Our battery supported the brigade operating in the division's southern area of operations, and even though we were routinely sent on missions throughout the Division's area of operations, we primarily flew missions in the southern area around such firebases as Rifle, Brick, Blitz, Normandy, Tennessee, Whip, and the notorious A Shau Valley.

The A Shau Valley was a fearsome place. It was located way out west near the Laotian border and seemed to be a favorite place for the bad guys to hang out. You may remember the 101st fought a big battle at a place called Hamburger Hill, located between the Valley and the border.

You could always rely on lots of enemy activity in the Valley. I always figured any time a commander at the Battalion level or higher needed another row of ribbons on his chest before his term of command ended, he would conduct an operation in the Valley. It was a happening place.

Every time we went to the A Shau Valley it was eventful. Once we conducted our only chemical warfare mission there when our entire battery participated in a mission where we fired only rockets with CS (tear gas) warheads. If I remember correctly it was not a roaring success and we never repeated that type of mission.

Another very interesting episode occurred in the Valley that involved a section from B Battery. A section is two aircraft consisting of the section leader and the wing man. It seems the section leader was shot down by enemy ground fire and the pilot was able to successfully put the aircraft down without injury to either of the occupants.

There were no friendlies on the ground near the crash site but there were lots of bad guys present. The wing man, Warrant Officer Frederick Cappo, made a quick decision to land and pick up his two buddies, since they were far from home in a bad neighborhood. There were several factors that made this an extremely hazardous decision.

The first difficulty was a Cobra gunship is only designed to carry two humans so they had to quickly decide where the passengers were going to ride. Also a Cobra is challenging to land, hover and take off in the best of circumstances. On top of this, they were surrounded by enemy troops.

In an act of incredible bravery, Cappo landed, popped off his window and started firing at the bad guys with the M-16 he always carried in the cockpit. The two downed pilots ran as fast as they could to the rescuing aircraft, followed by a hail of bullets hitting the dirt behind them. They both hopped up and straddled a rocket pod on either side of the aircraft facing the rear. It sounded like Roy Rogers hopping on Trigger.

The aircraft took off in a barrage of gunfire with the two rescued pilots clinging on for their lives to the rocket pods. Miraculously they made it back to safety. I was a little surprised the pilot of the rescuing aircraft only received a Silver Star for that unbelievable act of courage.

I was involved in a less gallant incident that left an indelible reminder with me. It happened as we were flying a fire mission in support of a downed Huey. Again the action was hot and heavy and the enemy was closing in for the kill. The folks on the ground requested we put rockets down closer than safety dictated. As we fired our rockets dangerously close to the downed aircraft, suddenly to my dismay I saw one of the rockets I fired was a flechette round.

Flechette warheads are referred to as nails because they are packed with hundreds of little metal shafts, each with a point on one end and a small fan on the other, and they have a strong resemblance to actual nails. As a matter of fact we frequently used the flechettes as nails for our building projects.

When those rockets are fired the flechettes scatter out like a shotgun blast to increase their lethality. Some of the flechettes from the rocket I fired spread out and hit the unfortunate pilot in the downed aircraft and destroyed his testicles.

Later when I was informed of this unfortunate development I was momentarily concerned for the injured pilot because if he did not already have children before the incident he was definitely not going to have any afterward. But I guess things like that occur in the fog of war. I was sorry it happened.

20 – ARA Missions

ARA or Aerial Rocket Artillery was a beautiful thing in Vietnam because it was so effective. It was more than just a good crowd chant. Earlier I mentioned the two primary missions of ARA were fire missions and landing zone preps. When properly utilized in those two missions, ARA had a tremendous impact on the outcome of combat situations. This was due to its prodigious firepower capabilities and its close-knit integration into the fire support communications systems. These two factors allowed us to rapidly bring a lot of firepower to a combat arena.

ARA fire missions were similar to tube artillery in how we answered the call of a forward observer requesting immediate fire support. In the 101st Airborne Division, as in the 1st Cavalry Division, artillery forward observers had an additional fire support asset available to them in the form of ARA. I mention the 1st Cavalry Division here because at the time there were only two airmobile divisions in Vietnam with ARA capabilities. The 1st Cav's ARA Battalion was the famous 2/20th Artillery with the impressive "Blue Max" moniker.

The ARA communications protocol would have impressed even Heinz Guderian. He was the signal officer in the German army during World War I who was instrumental in the application of effective radio communications in armored units. His work greatly enhanced the German Wehrmacht's ability to take over all those countries in World War II.

Artillery forward observers out with their infantry units had a direct communications link with their designated ARA support unit. That meant instead of having to go through numerous layers of command channels to request gunship support, help was available as soon as the push-to-talk button was pressed by the forward observer. That meant we could be putting rockets on a target as far away as the A Shau Valley within 10 minutes of receiving a call from an observer.

To maintain the ability of rapid response to a fire mission request, it was necessary to have a crew ready to go 24/7. That meant one group of pilots known as the "hot crew" had to be able to pull pitch (take off) within two minutes of a fire mission request. In our battery we had a small room to house this crew next to the flight line, where the four pilots would stand ready on hot status for 24-hour shifts. The hot crew was not allowed to leave the ready room except for fire missions. If that crew was called out on a mission, another crew would come over and assume the hot status duty.

Conditions in the A Battery ready room could be described as Spartan at best. My pilots and I spent many boring hours in that bare room furnished only with four uncomfortable cots and a small table. We would become desperate for any form of entertainment. One of the pilots had a small cassette player with one lone Moody Blues cassette. We would listen to the Moody Blues for hours on end. To this day I can remember every word of every song on that cassette and strangely enough, I still enjoy listening to the group. One of my other favorite diversions was reading every printed word in a Newsweek magazine. We also became very proficient in the card game of Spades. My career as a hatchet thrower began during those idle hours. Looking back I now, I think I should have been doing something useful as we awaited our next mission, like reading good books or quizzing the pilots on firebase locations.

Food for the crews on hot status would be delivered from the consolidated mess facility (for some unknown reason the Army refers to food as "mess"). Once I had a young pilot in my crew who obviously wasn't very bright. At Phu Bai all meals for the aviation units were prepared in one large, consolidated mess hall facility. It was formerly run by the Marines and they were apparently big on consolidation. Unfortunately this insured the food was not very appealing and the mess personnel were usually in unfriendly moods. Somewhere there must be a good reason for such a stupid policy as consolidated eating facilities.

Anyway, this dim-witted pilot would complain vigorously about the food to the driver who was kind enough to bring it to us. I had to explain to the young man it was not too smart to give a hard time to anyone bringing you food. I advised him he should be grateful to the delivery person and thank him very much. You don't want to rile them up. They may do something to the food during delivery or forget to bring it. Since we were all eating the same food I did not want to suffer from some other person's misguided actions.

The requirement for the aircraft to lift off within two minutes of receiving a fire mission request was a hard rule, but it had to happen. At first I was skeptical that it could be done but after a little practice I discovered it was fairly easy to do. We would sprint out to the aircraft and while the copilot was untying the main blade, the pilot would hop in the back seat, flip a few switches and light the fire. The copilot would hop in the front seat and strap in as the pilot pulled pitch and lifted off.

As you can probably assume, pre-inspection of the aircraft was very important to being able to takeoff within two minutes and be confident the ship would fly and the guns were loaded and ready for action. As we became more experienced in the art of quick departures, I was a little surprised at how easily it could be done. The old saying of "practice makes perfect" definitely applied here.

Taking off on a fire mission was when the fun really began. We would have no idea where we were going or what we were going to be asked to do as we were rushing to get into the air. As soon as we were airborne we would receive the mission briefing and it was the job of the front seat pilot to write it all down. Sometimes the mission information could be a rather voluminous so it was very important to have a front seat pilot who could write fast and legibly.

On occasion we would receive mission briefings so fearsome it would make a person want to look for mechanical malfunctions that would necessitate a return to base, but of course that never happened with me. We would first receive basic information about the mission, like contact details and locations, and then a description of the situation. This would be followed by information about friendly fire hazards.

A good example of these friendly fire hazards that comes to mind was during a memorable night fire mission where we were dispatched to Firebase Ripcord. The artillery advisory service informed us we could not enter three of the four quadrants around the firebase due to heavy incoming tube artillery fire, fighter aircraft operations, and B-52 bombing hazards.

After my first few fire missions I began to ignore warnings from the advisory service. My theory was big sky - small helicopter, and there was too much going on to worry about the probability of being hit by a stray artillery round. The only time I ever really paid much attention to artillery advisories was when some pansy wing man or front seat would complain and threaten to report me to the battery commander for being unsafe. After artillery advisories we would receive a briefing from the ground commander as to his situation and requirements. Many times on fire missions we would hear desperate requests that would always drive us to do everything possible to help the guys on the ground. On more than one occasion after we finished fire missions, we would get powerful messages of thanks, including a few "God bless ARA's," which I really appreciated.

The other ARA mission was landing zone preparations. These were quite different from fire missions. On fire missions we would essentially smash through the door and blow the hell out of everything in sight. Landing zone preps were more like a delicate ballet requiring lots of finesse. Fire missions required nerves of steel and dedication to whatever was necessary to accomplish the mission.

LZ preps required a different skill set than fire missions. Timing and positioning were critical. As opposed to fire missions, LZ preps were characterized by lots of planning and coordination. An LZ prep is an operation that assists in the successful conduct of an air mobile insertion of troops onto the battlefield.

There were several players involved in an LZ prep, including the operation commander who would always be somewhere far above, circling around in a command and control aircraft giving directions to all parties involved. Others included the escort gunships, the lift commander, and the artillery folks, to name a few.

The ARA's role in an LZ prep was to provide a final extension of the tube artillery preparation, meaning our job was to fire rockets on the LZ or selected areas nearby for a period of two minutes, beginning with the arrival of the last artillery round and ending when the first Huey touched the ground. As a safety precaution we would attack on a line perpendicular to the flight path of the lift ships. Our signal to begin firing would be a white smoke round delivered with the last artillery salvo. The artillery guys would give us a countdown to assist us in being in position at the correct time.

As we would be firing our LZ prep rockets, the lift company's organic gunships would be flying along with the lift ships and providing close support fire. The whole idea of an LZ prep operation was to provide as much support to the landing aircraft as possible. In some cases LZ preps would involve much more than tube artillery, ARA, and escort gunships. Sometimes you would see all sorts of Air Force assets involved, including prop driven fighters, F-4's, F105's, and sometimes even B-52s.

Preforming a successful ARA LZ prep mission was much easier said than done. I was amazed at the precise timing these missions required. They were not kidding when they said we had to put rockets on the target from exactly two minutes prior to touchdown, continuously until touchdown. It had to be done and nothing was more embarrassing than a failure to be in the proper place at the proper time. The lead gunship had to be in the exact position at the exact time ready to fire the first rocket. There were many things they would let slide in Vietnam, but LZ preps and fire missions were two of the things that absolutely had to be done right. Many times we would play around and have fun, but when it came time to perform these two missions it was all business. The reality of instant death will do that to you.

21 - Other Exciting Missions

I estimate more than 90% of our missions in Vietnam were LZ preps and fire missions. But on occasion we would receive other types of missions. One of the most common was flying escort for small scout helicopters known as "loaches" (Light Observation Helicopter). They would fly around like a bloodhound sniffing for targets and in the event they found something we would shoot at it. Luckily I did not have to fly many of these missions because they were a little boring and you know what the devil does with idle hands.

There was never a time on these recon cover missions where we fired on hostile human targets. But on more than one occasion we did find something to shoot at. In Vietnam there was an amazing array of animal life out in the countryside. Once on one of these boring missions the loach pilot spooked a large moose-like animal; it ran across a stream and hid its head in the brush on the far side and left the rest of its body exposed at the edge of the stream. I figured the animal thought if its head was hidden the rest of its body could not be seen.

I asked the loach pilot to clear the area and then advised him to get out of the way. Upon receiving clearance I laid down two or three pair of 10 pounders (rockets) on the beast and it was never seen again. We are not sure what happened to the moose but I believe it was immediately sent to moose heaven.

We had another incident with animals on one of those recon missions. This time it involved orangutans. We happened to be loaded with flechette rockets and they were not used on the mission. On the way back to our home base the loach pilot noticed a large group of orangutans. I figured since they were rather humanoid in appearance it would be a good opportunity to test the effectiveness of flechette rockets. Again I received clearance from the loach pilot and as my wing man circled above, I fired several pair of rockets on the herd and the deadly effectiveness of flechette rockets was verified by the loach pilot.

On another one of those recon support missions I exercised a little poor judgment. After finishing the uneventful mission I noticed a beautiful scene with a nice clearing next to a river. I gave into temptation and landed the section (two gunships) on the open space next to the river. We then proceeded to have a refreshing swim in the river. Fortunately there were no bad guys in the area and again the good Lord watched over us as we swam for a while and then got dressed, lit the fire, and returned to home base in time for one of those gourmet meals at the East Phu Bai Consolidated Mess Facility.

Another type of mission we would receive from time to time was a VIP orientation flight. For me it was sometimes more dangerous flying those missions than taking bullets through the canopy during an LZ prep. Once I was taking a high-ranking Engineer Corps officer for a short orientation flight and apparently he had heard of a maneuver called a "wingover" and he requested I perform one. They are not one of my favorite maneuvers because I liked living but he insisted, so I performed a rather weak example of one.

That was not good enough for him and he demanded I do a real wingover. That unfortunately got me started. I thought, Okay, you want a wingover? I will give you a wingover. I yanked that baby over further than I had ever done, way beyond safe limits. To get an idea how far I rolled over, if 12 o'clock corresponds to straight and level flying, we were turned over to about 5:30 on the clock. We were very close to being upside down and helicopters are not designed to fly that way.

The aircraft begin to vibrate, shake, rattle and roll. I was afraid my mother, Mrs. Payne, back in Central Florida might soon be receiving a letter from the Army about my untimely demise. But don't worry, I used all my flying skills and pulled out of the maneuver safely. The officer in the front seat immediately exclaimed, "That was fun - let's do another one." I respectfully declined and informed him our battery policy only allowed us to perform one of those maneuvers per day due to safety reasons. I think he believed me, as we continued the rest of the orientation flight uneventfully.

CCN missions were the most mysterious nonstandard operations we conducted. Command and Control North was located up north at Quang Tri and was made up of all sorts of clandestine elements like the Special Forces, Air America, and other assorted intelligence assets who remained nameless. The 101st Airborne Division was tasked to support CCN missions when needed. Elements from all the division's aviation units would be required to supply helicopter assets upon request.

CCN missions always evoked mixed reactions. Normally the missions would last no more than one day and they always provided us with excellent food. Many times we would sit all day and not go anywhere, so we had lots of time to play Spades, our favorite card game. Everyone would gather around and watch in amazement as Big Jim Fadden would set his opponents with every hand. It also gave everyone the opportunity to talk shop with other division aviation units we did not normally work with.

Whenever we did go out on CCN missions, they would take a large gaggle of aircraft including Hueys, Cobra gunships, Air Force FACs, and on occasion, propeller driven fighters. Most of the time we did not know where we were going or all the details. About the only thing I can remember about those missions is that we would go out of country and retrieve bodies.

There was a degree of urgency to some of the missions and we would go regardless of the time or weather. Once we took off in very bad weather that was certifiable IFR (Instrument Flight Rules) conditions and if you remember, earlier I mentioned most US Army helicopter pilots only received a minimum of instrument flight training. Many of the pilots had difficulties and we began to hear several of them reporting they were lost in the clouds and asking for help. Amazingly, we did not lose any pilots. However, many were scattered all over the place. Some headed east toward the South China Sea where they knew they would not hit a mountain as they descended. Others climbed over the bad weather and waited until a clearing appeared to locate the package, or go back to base at Quang Tri.

The mission commander persevered on with the remaining aircraft and we picked up another dead body somewhere out in the Kingdom of Laos. As we returned to the CCN base at Quang Tri it was dark, raining, and the visibility was limited to less than one mile. That was one occasion where I was very glad I had a standard instrument card.

Upon our return to Quang Tri, it was reassuring to find all the birds that had been scattered out in the bad weather had returned safely home to the chicken coop. Even though it was dark and raining, the flight home to Phu Bai was a pleasure.

CCN missions were okay but I always preferred to be with regular Army units and personnel. There were a lot of strange characters at CCN. There were personnel in both uniform and civilian attire who didn't talk much, and many appeared to be of foreign origin.

Speaking of strange people, I always got a kick out of the Air America guys. It was always hammered into us as military aviators that there were certain procedures we must follow or we would die. For instance, helicopters should not hover higher than three feet above the ground and we should wear long-sleeved clothing with gloves at all times.

Occasionally an Air America Huey would come into one of our refueling points and it was interesting to note the pilots would be dressed in white short sleeve shirts and would be flying barehanded. They would also hover anywhere between 10 and 20 feet above the ground. I thought to myself, they are setting a terrible example. But I believed most of the things the Army instructors told us had a margin of error built in. That's one of the reasons I figured it was okay to exceed the maximum do-not-exceed speed while diving. On many occasions I proved that you can exceed the maximum do-not-exceed speed by 20% and live to talk about it later.

22 - Lam Son 719

Without a doubt the biggest operation I was involved in during my flying year in Vietnam was Lam Son 719. Our battery moved out to Khe Sanh and operated in support of the South Vietnamese Army for six weeks as it plunged into the heart of the Ho Chi Minh Trail. I saw more real live combat action in those six weeks than in both tours combined. Everything before and after was anti-climactic.

It is helpful to know that eight or nine months prior to this operation the U.S. Army invaded the North Vietnamese Army sanctuaries in Cambodia. This invasion was designed to destroy military supplies accumulated for a suspected assault on the capital of South Vietnam. It was successful in the mission of capturing and destroying enemy war making matériel, but it caused a tremendous public relations challenge for President Nixon, who had ordered the move. The Kent

State tragedy resulted from the violence wrought by student opposition to the Cambodian incursion.

Military planners were pleased with the results of the incursion into Cambodia and concluded another such operation further north could fetch similar benefits. It was decided by military planners the second invasion would follow Highway 9, which ran across the northern part of South Vietnam from Quang Tri through Khe Sanh, and eventually out to the Laotian town of Tchepone and beyond.

This time only South Vietnamese troops would cross the border into Laos so as not to rile up American college students and cause additional Kent State type episodes. The Americans would be involved in it up to their necks with ground support extending out to the border and aviation support, which included us in A Battery, going with the South Vietnamese as far as they could push into the Kingdom.

In Vietnam at the time it was very hard to keep a secret. Consequently information about the proposed incursion into Laos was only known at the highest levels of government in the US and South Vietnam. The reality of the proposed action came as a surprise to the forces that were to take part. This led to some mistakes being made by the South Vietnamese forces who were nominally in charge of the invasion.

The South Vietnamese ran their part of the operation in their typical uninspired manner. Most of the higher ranking commanders very seldom visited the area and attempted to run their part from headquarters back in Saigon or Quang Tri. The overall South Vietnamese commander was named General Lam. In deference to him and the Vietnamese government the name of the operation, Lam Son 719, was derived from the general's name and the year 1971 in which it occurred.

In late January of 1971 our battery commander, Major Mills, informed us we would shortly be supporting the South Vietnamese Army in a large operation in the northern part of the country. We were surprised to learn our battery had been selected as the one unit from our Battalion to relocate to Khe Sanh. It would be a big change for us because we very seldom ever spent a night away from our home base at Phu Bai.

But this time the entire battery, less a few administrative personnel, was moving out lock, stock and barrel to this mysterious place in the mountains. It had the ominous reputation of being the place where the Marines had been rudely treated by the North Vietnamese Army three years earlier. The Marines had to be rescued by none other than the famous 1st Cavalry Division in Operation Pegasus. I figured our battery was chosen to move out to Khe Sanh because of our battery commander, the capable Major Mills.

Little did I know what lay ahead for us. Up until that time I had never participated in a truly large military operation in Vietnam. This one was definitely large, and overwhelming in its magnitude. One day at the very beginning, I was sent to LZ Evans where there was a landing strip and I was rather shocked to see 10,000 American troops standing on the runway with their equipment. We landed our gunships nearby to await further instructions. In a short period of time hundreds and hundreds of Hueys arrived at the landing strip and in just a few minutes all 10,000 of the troops were taken away by those Hueys. It was a most impressive demonstration of air mobility.

The mission of all those troops from the 101st was to secure Highway 9 leading out to Khe Sanh and the border. Some of those troops were sent to the A Shau Valley to create a diversionary action and provide cover for the South Vietnamese invasion a little further to the north.

Army assets from all over Vietnam were moved north to support this big operation. Even the vaunted 2/ 20th, Blue Max ARA from the 1st Cavalry Division came up to Khe Sanh from way down South. To me it was almost like a flight school class reunion because I saw so many of my classmates up there.

One of the many things that impressed me about Lam Son 719 was how the Army engineers rebuilt Highway 9 where it ran through some very rough mountains. It had been neglected since the Marines pulled out of Khe Sanh three years before and it was in bad shape. The engineers rebuilt about 20 miles of road through the most difficult and hostile terrain in just a few short days, and then proceeded to prepare the Khe Sanh base itself for the arrival of the Army units. This was no small task because the Khe Sanh perimeter was about two miles in diameter.

Unfortunately for me, my first day of Lam Son 719 turned out to be a day of shame. I mentioned earlier I had gained a reputation as a competent navigator because of my ability to quickly locate fire bases and find locations on the map.

For that reason I was selected to sit in the front seat of an aircraft piloted by Warrant Officer J.C. Borom. He was an excellent pilot and this turned out to be extremely fortunate. We were leading a package containing our entire Battalion of 18 gunships that was supposed to participate in the opening preparation fire for the occupation of the Khe Sanh firebase.

As luck would have it I happened to be having a bad day as a map reader. I misread the map and proceeded to lead the entire package over the corner of North Vietnam itself. The error in my navigation was first indicated by a sudden wall of red tracers appearing directly to our front. Warrant officer Borom executed a textbook wing over maneuver which more than likely saved us from instant death.

We quickly turned the package around and headed south. Before long we were able to see signs of intense aerial activity to our south. We soon learned they decided to carry on the party at Khe Sanh without us. There were many Army gunships and Air Force bombers prepping the area without our help. We arrived just in time to finish up the preparation festivities.

I was so ashamed of my navigation failure I avoided direct contact with Major Mills for several days thereafter. I was afraid he might demonstrate his karate skills on me. We did safely arrive at our new home and started setting up shop for the next six eventful weeks.

The history books will tell you this about the Lam Son 719: initially the South Vietnamese Army achieved an element of surprise that allowed them to move into Laos as far as Tchepone. The town was about 40 miles inside the Laotian border and the South Vietnamese stayed close to the road and the valley it ran through, and consequently had long, exposed flanks along their route of attack.

In a short time the North Vietnamese Army reacted to the invasion and proceeded to beat the stew out of the hapless South Vietnamese. This development provided me and the intrepid pilots of A Battery all the combat action we could hope for. In the next six weeks we would have the opportunity to rock em' and sock em' with everything from 2.75 inch aerial rockets, to six shooters and hatchets.

23 – The Khe Sanh Neighborhood

To a Florida flatlander the terrain around Khe Sanh was spectacular. The Khe Sanh firebase was located on a high plateau ten miles east of the Laotian border, 40 miles west of Quang Tri, and about 15 miles south of the DMZ. It was surrounded by mountains and bounded on two sides with a canyon featuring sheer cliffs.

It was high enough that clouds would roll in and create visibility conditions where you could not see your hand in front of your face at arm's length. The weather guys said it was heavy fog but I believe it was actually clouds because I had never seen fog so thick.

The Khe Sanh firebase was fairly large as firebases go. Its central feature was an airfield big enough to accommodate C-130s. There was still junk lying around from when the Marines had occupied the area, but the Army engineers cleared it away and quickly rebuilt the landing strip with PSP (pierced steel plank). It was interesting that only fixed wing aircraft could use the runway because when a helicopter hovered over the runway the down wash would cause the PSP to lift up like a tidal wave.

The Air Force set up a control tower to manage the huge amount of air traffic using the runway. At one time it was said that airfield was one of the busiest airports in the world. C-130s were continuously landing and taking off.

Our battery area was located north of the main runway near the perimeter on the northeast side of the firebase. We had our own little piece of the firebase that accommodated our six gunships, plus living and workspace for battery personnel.

The refueling point for rotary winged aircraft was on the south side of the runway. This created an interesting situation because we were not allowed to hover across the runway after refueling, due to the heavy fixed wing traffic.

There was a deep river gorge on the east and north side of the perimeter. We were instructed to proceed to the east end of the runway after refueling and descend into the gorge and pass underneath the runway flight path. This encouraged a little reckless flying on my part because I had the tendency to do a steep dive off the end of the plateau, circle around under the runway flight path, and after hitting max speed, head straight for the wall of the gorge and execute a cyclic climb up the face of the cliff. I always ended up with barely enough airspeed to reach the top of the plateau north of the runway. It was fun to scare the pants off new front-seat pilots with this maneuver.

Sometimes nerves would get a little frayed due to the busy air traffic. The Air Force tower personnel controlled all flights on the firebase, including rotary wing traffic to and from the refuel point. We could not move out of the refuel point without clearance from the tower. Sometimes we helicopter pilots got the feeling we were forgotten by the tower personnel.

I remember on one occasion a Huey pilot at the refueling point felt the controller had forgotten about him after he'd made a request to relocate. He indicated that to the controller in the tower, who apparently was too busy to address the pilot's request. The pilot began to express his views to the controller in more forceful terms. Soon each was challenging the other to a fist fight. It got so bad the pilot lifted up, flew over to the tower and set down, and settled the argument with fists.

Our living conditions at Khe Sanh were rather spartan. We were living in tents and crude sheds erected in a haphazard manner. Luckily for us Captain Fadden had the foresight to bribe a bulldozer operator from the engineers with a bottle of Jim Beam and had him create several large holes big enough to accommodate our GP Medium tents. This proved to be a fortuitous move. Later on the NVA was able to drag some artillery guns near enough to lob a few rounds inside the perimeter. There is nothing better than the sound of shrapnel flying through the top of your tent, instead of through the sides.

One of the most enjoyable aspects of moving out to Khe Sanh was the food. We were able able to pull our own cooks out of the big consolidated mess facility at Phu Bai and bring them with us. They were headed up by an old time mess sergeant who really knew how to put out good food. He was an excellent leader who could get the most out of his cooks, and no one had any complaints. The Army always kept us well fed.

The bathing facilities at Khe Sanh were nonexistent. I discovered one of the laws of nature about taking a bath. It is called "The Three-Week Rule." After three weeks with no bath it ceases to be uncomfortable and you get used to the BO. One of our hot shot pilots, Warrant Officer Ronnie Pepper, would hang up his flight suit on a stick at night and spray it down with Right Guard deodorant.

One day a few of us heard about the existence of a small waterfall over on the side of the gorge near the end of our landing pad. It was further reported to be a good place to take a shower, so several of us decided to give it a shot. We carefully climbed down along the side of the cliff with soap in hand and sure enough there was a small stream of water falling in such a manner you could stand under it and take a shower.

We were a little surprised to see others already using the facility. Some appeared to be Vietnamese and we figured they must be members of the South Vietnamese Army. We proceeded to use the facilities for a refreshing shower and restart "The Three-Week Rule." The wary Warrant Officer Pepper refused to use the waterfall shower, claiming it was unsafe.

Later after we had used the waterfall shower facility we began to muse as to who those Vietnamese were taking showers. After doing a little checking it was discovered there were no South Vietnamese Army units at Khe Sanh at that particular time, and there were no civilians in that area due to active combat going on. The only thing we could conclude was that we were taking showers with North Vietnamese Army soldiers. I always refer to that incident as the "Great Shower Truce."

A section of Cobras heading for battle

A Battery Cobras at Khe Sanh

Cobras in the rain at Khe Sanh

Junk we found at Khe Sanh

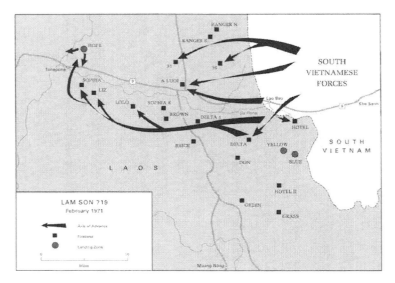

Lam Son 719 Battle Map

24 - Dining in the Rough

Earlier I made note of the fact that when we moved out to Khe Sanh, we were able to take our organic mess personnel with us. That turned out to be one of the most pleasant surprises of our Lam Son 719 adventures. The leader of the cooks was right out of the textbook on how to be a good mess sergeant.

With little to work with he and his staff provided the battery with excellent food. He was a crusty old guy who not only knew how to cook but how to get the most out of his crew. He operated out of a tent very near the perimeter. On the night we were paid a visit by the bad guys who passed by his area, without missing a beat he and his cooks put down their spatulas and picked up their M-16s and had at it with the little guys in black.

The mess sergeant was dedicated to taking care of us with good food. I remember one occasion when my crew and I were treated to some haute cuisine due to special circumstances. We were out on a late mission and I called back to request they inform the mess sergeant to save us something to eat. That particular night the featured entrée was smothered steak with roasted onions.

They saved us the leftover steaks in a large cooking pan. The pan was about 12" x 36" x 4" and they filled it with the steak, gravy, and roasted onions. For the convenience of the KP's it was placed on top of a large garbage can. In case we did not make it back in time, the food was close to where it would be dumped.

We made it back and rushed over to the mess tent as soon as we shut down. They directed us to the pan on the garbage can and we proceeded to tear into those steaks, all standing around the pan resting on top of the the garbage can. We enjoyed that food as much as if we were dining at the Waldorf-Astoria. It was a real morale booster to have such good food and service while we were roughing it out at Khe Sanh.

Although the food was good, the dining facilities were rather sparce in nature. Actually they were non-existent. In the beginning it was like eating at a picnic where there were no tables. Everyone would either stand or sit on the ground while eating.

After a few days of this I reasoned there must be a better way and decided to create a dining facility for my pilots and me. I asked for volunteers to assist in the project and none came forward. This caused a little rancor on my part toward my fellow aviators. It even caused me to refer to some as being dilatory louts with questionable parentage.

I resolved to do it myself and rounded up a crew chief to assist in the project. Not wanting to appear braggadocious I can't help reporting that the results were magnificent. With a little help from our Engineer buddies I was able to procure a large wooden cable spool that made a perfect dining table when turned on its side. Seats were made from ammo boxes and it was set up next to a CONEX container which supported a cover made from a large piece of unused canvas.

The acrimony that arose out of the creation of the dining table caused a humorous situation. When it was completed I proudly brought a plate of that delicious food and gracefully sat down at my new and comfortable dining table. The lazy naysayers, not daring to join me, sat down in the dirt with their food next to my luxurious new digs as I dined in style.

At first we silently stared at each like a pack of wild dogs getting ready to attack. You could almost here them growling with resentment because they had to eat in the dirt while I was enjoying a more civilized dining experience. After having a little fun with them for not helping build the facility, I finally invited them to join me and all was forgiven, even though I still considered most of them to be a little on the lazy side.

Another incident happened at my dining facility that I hate to mention but it is a part of my Vietnam Veteran Memoirs, so here it is. Our battery had its own area at Khe Sanh that was supposed to be our private little compound with landing pads, maintenance shops, sleeping areas, and headquarters.

Khe Sanh was a crowded and busy place with lots of strangers coming and going all the time. One morning a "blind tom" pilot who was new to the area had the audacity to land adjacent to my first class dining facility. I had just sat down with a super breakfast comprised of a big pile of perfectly scrambled eggs with a large rasher of tasty bacon, and a tall stack of pancakes drowning in butter and pure cane syrup that would put anything from IHOP to shame.

As soon as the errant Huey landed, the prop wash began to blow away my wonderful breakfast. First the pancakes began to fly away one at a time, followed by the scrambled eggs, and finally the bacon disappeared. In a very short time my entire breakfast was gone. I was splashed with cane syrup which collected much blown dirt upon my person.

I was totally incensed. In the first place he was not supposed to land in our area, especially near the mess tent. It just so happened to be one of those rare days when I was wearing a sidearm (a .38 revolver that was incapable of hitting anything more than 10 feet away). I was so mad I walked up to the pilot sitting in the aircraft, pulled my sidearm, stuck it in his face, and screamed he was not supposed to land on this spot and that he had ruined my breakfast.

Of course he could not hear a word I was saying over the engine noise and just stared at me in amazement. After calming down a little I holstered my trusty sidearm, wiped the syrup off my face and went back to the mess tent for a refill after the intruder had departed.

25 – The Media at Khe Sanh

There was always a great deal of media presence in Vietnam during the entire time of the major American involvement. During that period, Vietnam was always a front page issue both in print media and on TV news. The previous American incursion into Cambodia had been a very big news event. When word got out about another such operation in another country, it seemed like every media agency in Vietnam was drawn to Khe Sanh like bears to honey.

It was a real education for me to see this phase of the news production process. The old saying of "you do not want to watch sausage being made" could very well apply to the making of the news.

Reporters of every description descended like flies in July upon the firebase at Khe Sanh. Most of them hitched rides with Vietnamese aviation units since most American military personnel held reporters in low regard, and would do little to help them move around so they could write derogatory stories about the Americans.

The news correspondents ranged from the scruffy independent contractors all the way up to major news organizations like CBS and NBC with their sophisticated news gathering equipment.

I had the opportunity to chat with Jed Duvall who at the time was a big-time correspondent for CBS. I had seen him many times on TV and had the feeling I was talking to a real live celebrity. He was highly opinionated but a nice guy, and we had a long visit. I thought we saw eye to eye, but later he wrote a fairly uncomplimentary article about what we were doing up in the clouds at Khe Sanh.

In our conversation I learned some interesting historical facts. He explained some of the weirdness of the situation in Vietnam and how it came to be. It seems during World War II when the Japanese occupied present-day Vietnam, the United States enlisted the aid of local nationalists to fight against the Japanese. One of those nationalists enlisted to help the US was none other than Ho Chi Minh himself, who proved to be a valuable ally in helping us fight the Japanese.

According to Duvall, Ho Chi Minh received assurances from the American government he would be allowed to rule an independent Vietnam after the war. When World War II ended there was the absurd situation of Vietnam still being occupied by Japanese forces who had no way to return to Japan. France, the former colonial ruler, was unable to retake control of the country and the indigenous Vietnamese were not capable of running the country at the time.

Being the winners of World War II the Americans, after surveying the situation, instructed the occupying Japanese forces to stay in Vietnam and run the national government on a temporary basis. The Japanese remained there until 1946 whereupon they were returned to their homeland and control of Vietnam was turned over to Ho Chi Minh.

This was fine until 1947 when the Cold War began in Europe. France was an integral part of the effort to stem the expansion of the Soviet Union across Europe. As France began to recover from the devastation of World War II and attempt to reassemble it's colonial empire, the French began to lean on the US for assistance in regaining control of its colonial possessions, one of which was Vietnam.

In the case of Vietnam, the US was on the horns of a dilemma. It either had to:

1) Honor its promise to Ho Chi Minh for Vietnamese independence or,

2) Keep France as an ally against the expansion of the Soviet Union by allowing it to retake its former colony.

Unfortunately for Vietnam, the United States elected to back France and allow them to retake control of Indochina, which included Vietnam. The reporter went on to tell how salt was rubbed in the wounds of Ho Chi Minh and the Vietnamese people when at an international conference, American Secretary of State Dean Acheson turned his back on Ho Chi Minh and refused to speak to him. This is a tremendous insult to an Asian.

This conversation cleared up many questions in my mind as to how this Florida Flatlander ended up in a shoot-up in Southeast Asia. Ho Chi Minh was not so much a communist as he was a nationalist. He wanted independence for his country and he found a path to that end as a communist. It also became clear why there was no love lost between the US and Ho Chi Minh. We had stabbed him in the back and insulted him. The means justified the end.

Getting back to the "war correspondents," it was interesting to me how they were allowed a free rein to go wherever they wanted and make their uncensored reports. I think some of them reported more of their opinions than news. Jed Duvall's reports always seemed to be tainted with his negative opinions of the Vietnam situation.

It was fascinating to me that most of the reporters were only paid when they had their reports published in articles and they were compensated on a per-word basis. I always thought that practice might have influenced the news we received, but I guess that is the way the business worked.

Most of the reporters were good people but there were a few who could not qualify as such. Some were rather nasty individuals. I especially remember one particular female reporter who was not just another pretty face. She was rude, coarse, and overly offensive. It tested my belief in forgiveness and compassion when we heard she and some of her colleagues hitched a ride with a Vietnamese Huey that was shot down and they all died.

In the early stages of Lam Son 719 there were reporters everywhere. Several of our guys were interviewed on camera when they returned from missions, and after their three minutes on camera they would strut around like they were celebrities.

Unfortunately I missed my chance for fame because I was never selected for an interview under the lights.

The presence of the reporters added a little excitement to Lam Son 719 because it indicated to us we were participating in something historic.

26 – Flying in Hell

Flying Lam Son 719 missions in Laos was much different from what we were accustomed to back down south at Phu Bai. Activities there were far less demanding time-wise, and we seldom encountered intense anti-aircraft fire. Many times we would go days without a mission other than training. There was plenty of time to throw bayonets and go the 85th Evac Hospital Officers Club.

All that changed when we moved to Khe Sanh. From day one and until the South Vietnamese leadership declared victory six weeks later, we were thrust into a whirlwind of deadly combat. The array of weapons employed by both sides made me feel like the two national governments were putting on a display of every weapon of war they had short of nuclear for my personal benefit.

In the past I had been to many firepower demonstrations and seen lots of weapons from the Army and Air Force on display. Apparently, a few weapons were saved for special occasions like Lam Son 719. Sometimes I felt like a kid in a candy store looking at all the new things I had never seen before.

I was totally fascinated by what I saw there. It was the first and only time I had ever seen hostile tanks in combat that were shooting at us. Actually all the tanks I saw were PT-76 models that were not much more than beefed up personnel carriers, but they still carried guns that could pack a deadly punch.

The bad guys employed World War II style flak guns that made the sky look like scenes out of the Gregory Peck movie Twelve O'clock High. Fortunately those guns were designed for high flying aircraft and as long as we stayed below 10,000 feet AGL (above ground level), we did not worry about them except for a little metal that would fall down and cause blade strikes.

They also had lots of 12.7 and 37mm antiaircraft guns that made flying below 5,000 feet AGL somewhat hazardous. Some of the weapons manifested themselves with red tracers. I remember on one occasion the tracers were so thick I felt like a red shower curtain had been pulled completely around my aircraft.

One positive thing about tracers was they provided good reference points to shoot at. As long as we could stay between 5,000 and 10,000 feet AGL we were safe. I became proficient at making steep dives at high altitudes. Firing from higher altitudes helped me come back for another day of shooting rockets.

Something else we had never encountered at Phu Bai was incoming artillery fire from Russian-made 152 mm howitzers. The North Vietnamese were kind enough to let us observe the effects of incoming artillery close-up.

At first it appeared as if the Three Stooges were manning their artillery. For a day or so all the rounds landed on an open plateau outside the perimeter in plain view and only about half would detonate. The others would land harmlessly and sound like a rock hitting a pig sty.

Either they were poor artillerymen or are they were carefully registering their guns. Whatever the case, they finally got their act together and one morning about six o'clock, just as we were about to arise and greet the day, we heard the unfamiliar sound of artillery rounds whistling in just like I had heard in old war movies.

My pilots and I were sleeping in a GP Medium tent that was in defilade (arranged to be protected from enemy fire) up to its eave heights in the hole Captain Fadden had conveniently provided for us. As the rounds began to fall nearby, shrapnel started flying through the roof of the tent. One of the pilots zipped his sleeping bag all the way to the top thinking that would protect him and another started pulling sandbags on top of his sleeping bag.

I reassured them by letting them know we did not need to worry unless a round landed inside the hole where our tent was located. I attempted to calm them down by gently explaining either we would all die instantly, or it would soon pass and we would be enjoying some delicious pancakes in the mess tent in no time.

Dozens of rounds impacted in our area that morning. Many hit the landing pad where all six of our gunships were parked. I went out to survey the situation, fearing the worst. The ground was covered with freshly made shrapnel that was so sharp you could not pick it up with a bare hand safely, or walk without stepping on it. I thought every one of our aircraft would be damaged or destroyed.

Much to my amazement after looking at every aircraft, not one had any damage resulting from the incoming artillery fire. It was further revealed our battery had suffered no significant damage from the hostile artillery fire. The attack lasted a few days and I began to consider it a rather macabre joke because despite the terror of its appearance, it did very little damage. I thanked my lucky stars the NVA utilized unsophisticated fusing technology. Had they put VT (variable timer) fuses on those rounds we would have been in a world of hurt. I became rather amused at their pathetic efforts.

The only casualty suffered in our Battery from the incoming artillery fire was a crew chief who decided to watch the impact of incoming rounds from the doorway of his bunker. Unfortunately for him a piece of deadly shrapnel hit him in the hand. The wound was bad enough to send him to the rear for additional treatment.

One disappointment I had from the incoming artillery was our failure to employ a little ARA counter battery fire. I suggested such an endeavor to Major Mills but for some reason the usually aggressive commander demurred on the issue.

Our side too provided me with some special Lam Son 719 entertainment, mostly by the Air Force. F-4 Fighters that were originally designed for sophisticated warfare against other such aircraft were frequently used in Vietnam to support small ground unit operations. In Laos they dropped bombs that made the biggest Fourth of July fireworks displays pale in comparison.

One of the more impressive munitions dropped by these fighter planes was a cluster bomb. The main bomb would fall, explode, and then disburse smaller bomblets over a large area. Then each of those would explode, creating its own fireworks display.

Another effective tool used by the Air Force was smoke bombs, unlike any I had ever seen before. They were so effective they could completely hide 10,000 troops with clouds of opaque smoke. These smoke bombs came in very handy as the South Vietnamese withdrew from the incursion into the Kingdom of Laos.

Last but not least has to be one of the most awesome methods of firepower known to man. It was delivered by the old faithful B-52 bombers. These powerful, long-range strategic bombers were also used in Vietnam to support ground unit operations. They executed their support role with Arc-Light bombing missions featuring three B-52's flying in a V-shape formation.

Arc-Light bombing runs seemed to go on forever. Each bomber carried 30 tons of explosives and seeing all those bombs falling and exploding appeared to me as a scene from Armageddon. There is no doubt in my mind that short of nuclear weapons, Arc-Lights were the most awe-inspiring displays of firepower I had ever seen. I had never seen an Arc-Light mission before flying into Laos and it left an indelible mark on my memory.

My introduction to Arc-Lights was a little humorous. They would be announced by a radio warning on the guard channel that overrode all other radio transmissions. It must have been broadcast by ultra high-powered transmitters because it was always loud and disturbing and would disrupt any radio conversations being conducted at the time of its broadcast.

The Arc-Light warnings would be introduced by a deep-voiced individual blasting out the announcement:

"THIS IS HILLSBOROUGH ON GUARD - for the next 10 minutes stay out of the following coordinates."

He sounded like God calling out from above and would then read off several lines of coordinates. I found this to be so disturbing I began to turn off the guard channel on my radios. It was hard enough comprehending traffic from four different radio sources and I figured I could risk not listening to all those distracting warnings. Again I reasoned, large sky, small aircraft, and that made the possibility of being struck with a 1,000 bomb falling from a B-52 highly unlikely.

One day while flying near Firebase A Loui, I suddenly noticed my aircraft began to vibrate rather violently. My first thought was something was seriously wrong with the main rotor because the aircraft was producing low frequency vibrations. Quickly I checked all my gauges, looked up at the main rotor and then glanced out my right door and I had one of those "GOOD NIGHT NURSE AND CHE CHE BUG" moments.

An Arc-Light had just begun out my right window and was headed straight for us. I did not worry too much about being in their way because we were traveling perpendicular to the path of the falling bombs and I was confident we would clear the area safely. I was in awe of the most incredible sight I had ever seen. As each bomb detonated, I could see the shock waves emanate from the explosion. It remains a mystery to me how anything could live through an Arc-Light strike.

I was always grateful to the Air Force for putting some of their more lethal and effective weapons on display for me.

It was in this maelstrom of deadly combat that this Florida flatlander from a small town in the middle of the state found himself. Those six weeks were to be the ride of a lifetime and we could hardly wait for it to begin.

27 – Lam Son 719 Missions

The types of missions flown in Lam Son 719 were similar to the ones we had previously flown down south – fire missions and LZ preps. The big difference was the frequency and lethality of missions in Laos. From day one we were quite busy and for most of us it was exactly what we had been preparing and hoping for in the previous months of flying missions for the 101st. The challenges and dangers we faced were exhilarating for me to the max. We were able to shoot lots of rockets, which I never tired of doing.

In the early stages we primarily performed LZ preps as the South Vietnamese established their firebases. That was followed by a slew of fire missions as they become more engaged with the enemy and as they withdrew under pressure from their incursion into Laos.

It was fascinating to watch the Lam Son 719 operation unfold. In the fashion of many events in the Vietnam conflagration, it was planned and directed from the highest levels of national government, all the way down to specifying which infantryman could shoot someone, how, and when. One of the manifestations of this phenomenon was the use of the large CH-53 helicopters in Lam Son 719.

I was a little surprised to see these big and bulky aircraft being used to insert troops into hostile LZ's. Fortunately for our side this policy was stopped early on in the first few days. About the only tangible results apparent to me from using those ill-suited aircraft were more dead South Vietnamese troops and more junk on the battlefield for the scavengers. More than likely the North Vietnamese gunners hated to see them go because they made such easy targets to knock down.

Another outcome of this strategically planned maneuver was the demise of the C model gunship (a variant of the Huey). Earlier I mentioned that US aviation units from all over South Vietnam had been sent to Khe Sanh to participate in the duck shoot. Some of the units were equipped with the older C model gunships.

C model gunships were an earlier helicopter developed just prior to the faster and deadlier AH-1G Cobras we were using. They were a shortened version of the versatile Huey with a beefed up rotor system and weapon racks attached to each side. During takeoffs they would bounce along like fat geese struggling to get airborne. I got a kick out of our young crew chiefs diving for cover when a visiting C Model executed a takeoff from our landing area because it appeared to be in the process of crashing.

Unfortunately for their crews, C Models were not suited for the lethal environment of Lam Son 719. It can be said the entire inventory of C Model gunships was eliminated in the first few short weeks of the campaign. It was a terrible thing for the brave men who died as a result, because it forever changed the lives of the ones they left behind. But on the positive side, the US Army did not have to worry about mothballing all those obsolete gunships because they were all destroyed on the road to Tchepone.

The action for us in our Cobra gunships was hot and heavy from day one. While returning from our first mission in Laos we did some sight seeing through a scenic little valley. One of the pilots reported seeing personnel walking around in the open and requested permission to roll in hot on the suspected enemy. I denied the request thinking they may be civilians and we did not want to cause trouble by killing a bunch of Laotian farmers. I was remembering the trials of Captain Medina and Lieutenant Calley of My Lai fame. Much to my surprise these seemingly innocent Laotian farmers pulled the covers off over 70 Russian tanks and they all seemed to start firing at us at once with their 12.7's.

Unfortunately we had nothing for them. We were out of rockets and the type we normally carried were high explosives which would not kill tanks. I heard they quickly brought up anti-tank rockets that were given to the cavalry squadron. We in the ARA were a little insulted that the cav guys had all the fun of knocking out the enemy tanks. It was common knowledge that ARA pilots were the best rocket shooters. I figured the cavalry squadron commander must have been more persuasive than the artillery people and prevailed in getting first dibs on the anti-tank rockets.

Another aspect of this operation was the shared airspace. We had often seen Air Force planes in action before, but in Laos they seemed to be everywhere. The sky was full of A1 Skyraiders, which were prop-driven aircraft that reminded me of leftovers from World War II. There were lots of F-100 jets and of course the sexiest of all jet fighters, the F-4 Phantom. One F-4 could carry more than twice the bomb load of a B-17 bomber of World War II. Last but not least were the humongous B-52 bombers that were heard from but seldom seen.

Sometimes the airspace would get a little crowded. One day I was flying along straight and level in the vicinity of Firebase Lolo and suddenly an F-4 overtook me and passed by so close I could read the US Air Force logo written on its fuselage. Momentarily I was shaken up and a little miffed at the pilot for coming so close. I had to fight off the devilish desire to send a pair of rockets past his canopy as payback, but fortunately my better judgment prevailed.

Speaking of Firebase Lolo, one cloudy day we were involved in a particularly hair raising event near the firebase, which was situated on top of an escarpment (I picked up that addition to my vocabulary during Lam Son 719). I was flying on the wing of a gunship flown by PIC (Pilot In Command) Warrant Officer Sam Mitchell, who had Warrant Officer Tony Hoffman in the front seat. There were low hanging clouds that necessitated operating lower than we usually practiced, and just as we were about finished with the mission, I heard the dreaded call from Sam Mitchell - they were going down.

He was able to make a controlled crash landing on the side of a hill where both pilots were unharmed and able to safely exit the aircraft. The problem was, they were nearly surrounded by a host of NVA troops who were rapidly closing in for the kill. I was out of ammo and had to think fast. At first I could just see the medals I was going to receive for going in and picking up the downed pilots on my empty rocket pods, a la Warrant Officer Frederick Cappo of A Shau Valley fame. But that did not happen.

Two factors caused me to forgo such an effort. One, there were too many enemy troops in the immediate area. Had I landed there is no doubt I would have had company in the cockpit as soon as I touched down. Second, Sam had managed to put the aircraft down near a South Vietnamese firebase. There were friendlies nearby.

The only thing I could do was attempt to fake out the guys in black pajamas (the standard uniform of an NVA soldier) and occupy their attention long enough for the downed pilots to scramble up into the relative safety of the South Vietnamese firebase.

So there I was, a single aircraft, no ammo, under low hanging clouds, and my buddies were down and being threatened by a horde of bad guys. The only course of action left to me was to try to scare them off by the use of deception, a la Nathan Bedford Forrest. I decided to dive at the enemy and give them the impression I was going to blow them to hell. The first pass I made reminded me of a scene I once witnessed at the Lovers Key State Park near Fort Myers, Florida. The white sand beach had been covered with a multitude of small crabs so thick the white beach appeared black. As I walked towards the crabs, they drew back and the white sand magically reappeared as if a tarp was being pulled away.

I dove down toward the advancing enemy and went lower than I had ever dared, so low I could just about tell the color of their eyes. I aimed straight at the little bastards and they drew back just like the crabs on the beach at Lovers Key State Park. Oh, how I wished for just a few pair of seventeen pounders. I could have easily exceeded the kill record that day of our ace pilot Ronnie Pepper.

I pulled out of the dive and thought, hey, that worked pretty good and I am still alive, so let's try it again. It was so predictable. This time fewer of the little guys took the bait. About half of them ran and the rest stood there and watched. No offense to our battery maintenance officer, the ever-popular Captain Rick Scruggs, but very few of the chin turret guns worked on A Battery gunships, including the one I was flying that day. I had nothing for the enemy other than deception. I believe after the second pass the little fellers on the ground were beginning to realize I was putting the shuck on them.

On the third pass all hell broke loose. None of them ran away like crabs and they all stood fast and began shooting at me with all they had. This development, and the fact the downed pilots had made it inside the friendly firebase, caused me to conclude it was time for the widowed Mrs. Payne's young son to vacate the area.

Later that day the two downed pilots were picked up by a medevac helicopter and returned to our unit. We all gathered in the battery headquarters tent to recount the adventures of the day. Tony Hoffman was quite animated in his description of their ordeal and proudly displayed a North Vietnamese flag he had captured during his "down time." He recounted how he inadvertently picked up the flag as he reached out of a foxhole searching for a cloth to wipe his face. After grabbing the first linen object he could find he was surprised to discover it was an enemy flag. He decided to confiscate the pennant as a memento of his rough treatment. Both the downed pilots were unharmed and resumed their flying duties the next day.

Not all engagements with the enemy had such happy endings and some were downright sobering. I remember one particularly riveting LZ insertion where they were attempting to put a large number of troops in an area on a mountain top that could only accommodate one or two aircraft at a time.

The fleet of Hueys bringing in the troops had to line up in a single approach column so one aircraft at a time could land on the small LZ. The line of aircraft stretched out for miles. The procedures were carefully explained to the lift ships and the insertion began. The first helicopter in line began its approach and as it was about to land the pilot reported they were taking heavy ground fire. Immediately after he made that report the helicopter crashed headlong into the side of the mountain and exploded. That sight was enough to make a person have second thoughts about attempting to land on that LZ, but the next aircraft continued its approach and made it to the ground. As soon as it touched down its main rotor blade stopped turning and it sat there motionless where it landed. A third Huey landed with similar results. At that point the insertion was called off.

I cannot imagine the consternation that must have been felt by the Huey pilots as they were in line waiting for their turn to land, and watched the enfolding events. Never had I seen such bravery and felt so much admiration for those lift ship pilots. Sometimes Cobra pilots would think they were "hot stuff" but little could compare to the bravery of the pilots I saw that day.

Another sad event happened a short time later as we were supporting a withdrawal from an embattled firebase. It was a sizable operation with lots of aircraft engaged in the effort. The airlift commander in charge was emphatic in his instructions that aircraft must depart the LZ to the right side because of heavy anti-aircraft fire on the left.

The first helicopter departed the firebase to the left. I thought I must have heard the instructions wrong. I asked my front seat pilot to confirm the instructions to depart to the right. We both agreed the command was to depart right and as we were commenting on that point, the first departing helicopter exploded in air. It was obvious the airlift commander knew what he was talking about.

Seeing aircraft blowup like that is a very sobering experience. You knew the people on board were dead and I would think of how the lives of everyone close to the deceased airmen would be forever changed. I had an uncle who was killed on Iwo Jima in World War II. He left behind a widow, daughter, sister (my mother), and parents. His family never got over his death. Because of this I knew of the pain and suffering those untimely demises were going to cause many loved ones.

Again, I kept thinking all this could have been avoided if Walter Cronkite had not announced on national TV three years earlier that we lost the war after we beat the hell out of the little bastards during Tet of '68. The defeatism of Cronkite, Jed Duvall, et al., still makes me want to puke after all these years.

Another puzzling event occurred later as the South Vietnamese were "getting out of Dodge" in a rushed and emphatic manner. There was a nameless winding river running through the valley below the escarpments. A large number of helicopters were going to extract a force of South Vietnamese who were in a defensive position on one side of the river. They were under under heavy enemy pressure. The position was near a big U-shape bend in the river which was easily recognizable from the air.

This operation was so big, the Air Force was going to carpet bomb the large enemy positions on the opposite side of the river. Our battery was assigned to provide supporting fire immediately after the Air Force did their thing.

As we were in position and ready to go, the commander of the Air Force support aircraft, who was a talkative fellow, described in detail how his bombers were going to come in and cream the enemy so thoroughly the Army aircraft could easily go in and complete their mission. He informed us how the bombers were going to lay down their bombs precisely along the east side of the river where the bad guys were located.

He had us excited about how the bombers were going to perform so well. We all watched in anticipation as the fighter-bombers approached, and as the bombs began to fall, they started to fall on the west side of the river directly on the South Vietnamese positions.

We all watched in stunned silence as the poor South Vietnamese were blasted by the ill-placed bombs. At first I again wondered if I had heard the Air Force commander correctly. Sadly he was correct and the pilots missed their target with disastrous results.

After a long pause, the Air Force commander announced the pilots were out of fuel, ordnance and ideas. He then announced they were going home. After the Air Force fiasco the operation was called off so the damage could be assessed.

Not all the blood shed was in Laos. One particular grisly event happened uncomfortably near our battery headquarters. A Cobra gunship belonging to the Cavalry Squadron had been damaged by enemy fire out over Laos and was trying to limp back to Khe Sanh. The front seat pilot had been wounded so the PIC struggled to set the crippled gunship down at the aid station landing pad to get the injured pilot immediate treatment.

Had the pilot been smart enough to stop at that point and shut down the damaged aircraft on the aid station pad, he would have prevented a terrible accident. Cobras are challenging to fly under optimal conditions but without functioning hydraulics, they are nearly impossible to control. It was reported this aircraft had no hydraulics yet the pilot decided to attempt to lift off and fly over to his unit area.

It just so happened a large group of South Vietnamese soldiers were standing near our battery headquarters waiting to depart the area on incoming Hueys. The damaged Cobra flown by the unthinking Cav pilot crashed directly into the group of South Vietnamese and literally cut them to pieces with its flailing main rotor. It was a scene of unspeakable human carnage.

Several people from our battery were rocked by the commotion and ran to investigate, including Captain Scruggs. One of the unfortunate South Vietnamese soldier's body was severed into two parts at the waist. The top half of the torso was still alive and started crawling toward our guys. CPT Scruggs was heard to shout out, "Stay away, we want no part of you over here." Sometimes war can be shocking as hell and still provide platforms for a wit to display their talent.

I was very fortunate to survive the war without ever receiving a Purple Heart, although I did come close one time in Laos. In a situation much like that of a Stuka dive bomber pilot, I was making a steep dive between two mountains. I was taking fire from bad guys on the forward mountain side and my aircraft has hit in a strange place. A projectile hit the canopy directly on the top immediately to the rear of my seat and punctured the ECU (air conditioning) hose that looped just inches from my head.

On our return from the mission I reported the incident and the fearsome Major Mills came out to inspect the aircraft. After studying the entry point of the bullet he concluded I was flying upside down and proceeded to chew me out for not following proper helicopter flying protocol. I hoped he was kidding but with him you never really knew.

A TI (technical inspector) examined the aircraft and because the bullet had damaged the door frame he concluded it was structurally unsafe to fly. I informed him I was in a disagreement with his assessment but he insisted the aircraft was officially out of service. Not wanting to miss out on any of the fun going on in Laos I told him, "Watch this," and took off, headed west for the badlands.

The aircraft performed as it should except for one thing. The hole in the ECU hose allowed that ice cold air intended for cooling my seat to blow directly on the back of my neck. After two days of such comfort I came down with a head cold. If you have ever flown with a cold you probably noticed your ears hurt when the airplane descends.

It had always been drilled into us at flight school that you should not fly when you were congested with a cold. Since I did not want to miss any of the action I went against my better judgment and flew anyway. On the first steep dive of the day going from 10,000 feet to 5,000 feet in seconds, my head almost exploded inward with intense pain. I was surprised nothing broke in there.

After that experience I decided they knew what they were talking about in flight school in reference to flying with a severe head cold. I decided to take off a day or so.

So that is what I figure was my closest brush with earning a Purple Heart. If I had blown out my eardrums, I would have claimed I deserved the award because it was caused by the bullet that ripped the ECU hose that resulted in my miserable head cold.

I must relate another humorous incident involving the fearsome Major Mills. One day I was flying missions over Laos with Warrant Officer Barry Martens in the front seat. He was a fine young man who was new to the unit. I had already scared him a little with a hairy cyclic climb up the cliff face after refueling.

During a fire mission we took a jolting hit in the side of the aircraft directly under my seat. This was more than the hits I had taken before in the canopy that had sounded like small stones hitting the windshield of a car. I knew this was a little more serious.

I called off the mission and we headed home to check out the damage. We made it safely back to our unit landing area, and as I was shutting down the aircraft young Barry jumped out of the front seat and looked back at the damage. Suddenly his eyes widened, and his bright red hair stood on end as he screamed, "FIRE, FIRE! Get some fire extinguishers fast."

Since there were no apparent flames coming up around me I suspected he was overreacting, nonetheless I called the battery headquarters and requested someone bring a fire extinguisher because we may need one in a hurry. The battery headquarters was located about 75 yards from where I was parked and about one minute after my request I saw a Jeep with maybe eight people hanging on like the Keystone Kops coming my way at breakneck speed.

One of the passengers was Major Mills himself. I told him I was very impressed with their fast reaction to my request and as usual he had no comment. The reason for WO Martens alarm was fuel gushing out of a hole in our fuel tank, no doubt caused by the heavy projectile that had rocked the aircraft earlier. I still remember to this day the vision of the Jeep loaded with the Keystone Kops-like figures flying across the landing pad, coming to our rescue.

28 - Good Grief! They Are Amongst Us

The element of surprise was initially achieved in Lam Son 719 by the South Vietnamese Army but the North Vietnamese reacted quickly and brought in their big guns within a few weeks. In addition to roughing up the South Vietnamese and driving them out of Laos, they tried to put pressure on the Americans back at our big firebase at Khe Sanh.

That intention was first manifested with a few errant artillery rounds tossed our way. Toward the end of our stay at Khe Sanh they audaciously launched a night attack against the firebase. Our battery area was adjacent to the perimeter and one night an unknown number of enemy sappers penetrated the wire uncomfortably near us.

I called them sappers because the first thing they did was light up the ammo dump on the other side of the runway. It was a spectacular sight, outdoing any Forth of July fireworks display I had ever seen.

The ruckus began as my pilots and I were sleeping in the security of the fortified bunker we had built adjacent to the aforementioned GP Medium tent we formerly called home. As the situation had grown more hazardous we felt we needed more protection than a canvas tent could provide.

It never ceased to amaze me how the opposition always seemed to know as much about us and our equipment as we did. I remember during my first tour we could always find out when the military officials were going to issue new military pay certificates (legal tender in country) from the local Vietnamese vendors. It was supposed to be a super secret event but the little people always knew about it ahead of time.

Their ability to know about us and our equipment was displayed that night by the way they so easily disabled every one of our gunships except for mine, which they burned to the ground. The tail boom of a Cobra is secured to the aircraft frame with four bolts. There is a small inspection door about four inches square for checking the condition of the bolts. The sappers knew exactly where to go to do the most damage with the least amount of effort in the shortest period of time. Later we found the inspection door open on each aircraft where a small explosive charge had blown off the bolts. This caused the tail boom to drop two inches, making the aircraft unflyable.

They must have decided to make an example of my aircraft, which was parked only yards away from our sleeping bunker. Whatever they did, it was destroyed completely. The only thing left was the rotor head. Everything else was reduced to dust, including the 76 rounds in the rocket pods.

The first indication something was going on in our area was a nearby commotion that sounded like a flame thrower. By this time we had all awakened when the ammo dump began popping. We were lying in our sleeping bags wondering, what next? I commented to the boys, that noise sounded just like a flame thrower. Suddenly there was silence as we all began thinking the same thing. What if they aim the flame thrower into our cozy little bunker?

The silence was broken when Terry Martel, one of my favorite guys and who continually bummed cigarettes, asked me for one of my Marlboros from a soft pack (I mentioned the soft packs because the hard packs were for girls only). When he asked his voice was very shaky and sounded like he had just stepped into a house of horrors. I thought to myself, what a sissy - come on and man up, it's not that bad. I pulled out a Marlboro and handed it to him. Much to my surprise, I replied to him in an equally shaky voice.

We went outside to investigate and were met with one of those Dante's Inferno scenes from hell. The ammo dump was aflame with artillery rounds exploding and rockets firing off in all directions. Frequently an explosion would light up the area and we would see all sorts of strange people running around. It would have made a good movie scene.

This was one of those occasions I wished I had a weapon. I walked over to check my aircraft and was a little confused because it was not where I had left it a few hours before. That's when I stumbled across the rotor head and noticed during the next explosion the only thing left besides the rotor head was ashes.

I went back and rejoined my guys at our bunker. There wasn't much we could do other than watch this scene from hell. During an explosion we noticed a group of armed men running in one direction. In the next explosion we would see a different group of men running in the opposite direction. In some ways it was similar to a Bennie Hill show.

There was action going on everywhere. Even the crew chiefs and mess personnel were mixing it up with the bad guys. Luckily there was a platoon of infantry troops from the Cav Squadron who came over to lend a hand in smashing the flies.

As we were watching the scene unfold I was standing next to Phil Bergfield who had a .38 pistol with him. Suddenly a lone enemy soldier ran by like a rabbit. On the spur of the moment Phil said, "Let's go get him." In a momentary lapse of sanity I said, "OK, let's go," and the two of us sprinted off after the little jack rabbit.

As we were running as fast as we could after the intruder I began to think he was probably carrying dynamite and wondered about the wisdom of our actions. We continued the chase until Phil became a little winded and put a stop to this foot chase by shooting the enemy in the buttocks. That slowed him down considerably. He fell to the ground and we captured our first enemy soldier.

We secured him until he was taken into custody by the proper authorities. It was the first live NVA I had seen close up since we were taking showers with them on the side of the mountain. This one was much less friendly than the others.

After that bit of excitement we went back to the bunker and joined the others who were watching the action. Things began to die down as the invaders were systematically eliminated and the ammo dump was about burned out. As we stood and watched, something incredible happened.

Let me introduce you to Specialist Dula. He was one of our aircraft maintenance guys and was one of the most likeable people I had ever met. He was from North Carolina and was assigned as an armorer who worked on the weapon systems of our aircraft.

He reeked of friendliness and epitomized the term "good ole boy" with his smooth North Carolina accent and his characteristic easy gait. Every one liked Specialist Dula. This was demonstrated one day when he was in the process of disarming the guns of a chin turret on an aircraft that was going back to Phu Bai for repairs.

There were several people standing near the aircraft and I was walking toward it when the 40mm grenade launcher inadvertently fired a round as Dula was reversing the launcher cam. Everyone froze in disbelief and watched as the round sailed over a small hill inside the perimeter and exploded out of our sight with its characteristic "whump" sound.

After a short silence I said, "Maybe they will think it was incoming over where the grenade landed." I told everyone to scatter and forget the incident. To this day you the reader, Specialist Dula, and I are the only ones aware of what happened. The tribute to Dula is this - had it been anyone else he would have been reported. Someone could have been killed.

Now getting back to the incredible event, as we stood next to our bunker discussing the events of the evening, Major Mills appeared out of the darkness after he had been down by the wire and stated, "Dula is dead." He said it happened when a satchel charge was thrown into his tent.

We were shocked at hearing the news. I wondered, why did it have to be Dula? Not that we wanted to lose anyone, but it was a shame it had to be someone as likeable as Dula. We all moped around and expressed how we were going to miss his pleasant disposition.

Suddenly in another flash of light I thought I saw someone pass by walking in the familiar manner of Specialist Dula. Using my flashlight I confirmed to my surprise it was Specialist Dula. I could hardly believe my eyes because Major Mills was not prone to error, especially when reporting deaths.

We all were quite relieved and happily welcomed him back to the living. He was nonchalant about the affair and told us another soldier happened to be wearing one of his shirts and was unfortunately killed in the attack. Initially it was reported Dula had died because of the name on the shirt.

That poor unfortunate soldier was the only fatality our battery suffered in Lam Son 719.

It must have been awfully frustrating to the North Vietnamese. They attacked the US Army firebase at Khe Sanh, lost many soldiers, damaged a lot of equipment and materiel, and in a day most of it was replaced as if nothing had happened.

It really didn't matter much. We were about ready to pull out and go home to Phu Bai because our mission was coming to an end. I was wondering if all those dead NVA bodies were worth the effort. Again I go back to

Walter Cronkite's proclamation three years earlier that enabled this foolishness to continue and contribute to causing more dead bodies.

29 - Revelations from Observations

The six weeks we spent out at Khe Sanh supporting Lam Son 719 was a highly intense experience that helped me see and appreciate things from a different point of view. I will relate to you several revelations that came to me during that exciting time. They forever changed my thinking. One was political and another was psychological in nature.

The first revelation was geo-political in essence. On my first tour I had noticed early on things were not what I expected. Prior to my deployment to Vietnam, the Army expended much time, expense, and effort in training and preparing me for what I would face in the engagement.

About two weeks after my arrival at Camp Enari and assignment to the Fourth Infantry Division, I discovered the modus operandi was, This is Vietnam, we don't do that here, referring to the procedures we had been taught. Most of the body of knowledge I had learned previously was replaced with the resolution to do what was necessary to get out of there alive, enhance a resume, and stay out of the US Army stockade at Fort Leavenworth.

Once this awareness settled into my thinking I resolved to minimize worrying about the big picture and do the best I could at my assigned jobs, accumulate as much money in the 10% savings program as I could, happily anticipate the R&R's, and enjoy the entertainers from Subic Bay. I also became a world class tourist. It was my good fortune to have assignments requiring travel through the countryside where I could savor and enjoy the exotic Oriental culture and geography.

I carried this philosophy with me into my second Vietnam tour with the 101st Airborne Division. One day in Laos something happened that forever seared into my mind what a weird situation the widowed Mrs. Payne's young son had been thrust into.

Flying a Cobra gunship had its advantages. First was the air-conditioning system, which in typical Army jargon was referred to as the Environmental Control Unit (ECU). An ECU was necessitated by the fact Cobras had a sealed cockpit with no wind vents. Without a cooling system pilots would suffer heat strokes in no time.

The ECU was a source of envy among Huey pilots, who would have to endure hot temperatures in their open aircraft while watching a Cobra pilot hover by in air-conditioned comfort at a refueling point. The Cobra jock would many times be all decked out in a flight jacket, feigning shivers from the cold air blowing in his face. I guess someone had to do it.

The cockpit of a Cobra was rather cramped but it did provide space for a few amenities. One example was the barely adequate space for a Coke can on one of the side consoles. You had to be careful not to spill any Coke on the circuit breakers. It was very embarrassing to have to ask your crew chief to clean the circuit breaker panel.

You could also find room on a console for every pilot's favorite, a Hershey bar with almonds. And of course the handy little pocket on the sleeve of the Nomex flight suit was perfect for dining utensils and Marlboro soft packs. All macho Cobra pilots preferred Marlboros in softpacks.

Another nice amenity enjoyed by Cobra pilots was access to entertainment over the airways (this particular amenity was also available to pilots of other types of aircraft). Cobras were equipped with an ADF navigational receiver which had an AM frequency range that enabled tuning in the AFVN (Armed Forces Viet Nam) radio station and listening to the popular tunes of the day.

A big difference between my two tours in Vietnam was the AFVN radio programming. On my first tour they attempted to provide music for all ethnic and national groups. They had every thing from big band, to polka, to Hawaiian music, and they succeeded in satisfying no one. The most interesting thing I remember hearing on the radio that first year was the VC blowing up the radio broadcast station in Saigon while it was on the air. Now that was late breaking news!

I always assumed Wayne Burnside, the famous DJ with the signature sign-on GOOOOOOOOOOOOOOOOD MORNING VIET NAM and other station management personnel wised up and decided to play what everyone wanted to hear. On my second tour it was straight Rolling Stones and other such rockers. Thank goodness the polka music and Hawaiian ukeleles were no longer heard.

One bright sunny day I was flying about Laos engaged in rockin' and sockin' the bad guys. While shooting rockets and dodging tracers I was enjoying all the aforementioned amenities. They included a Marlboro between sips of Coke and bites of a Hershey bar, while listening to the latest tunes on AFVN.

Whenever you pull out of a steep dive in a Cobra you are under a heavy G force pressure that makes you feel like a giant hand is pressing you down into the seat. The aircraft vibrates violently as it breaks the momentum of the high velocity diving maneuver.

There I was, sipping on a Coke, munching a Hershey bar, puffing on a Marlboro Bob Dylan style, and listening to the Guess Who singing the song, No Sugar Tonight. I pulled out of a steep dive that would have impressed even Hans Rudel (famous Stuka dive bomber pilot).

It was during that pull out when I was hit broad side with a revelation. I could clearly realize the insanity of what we were doing. Here I was sending little guys to the big rice paddy in the sky while enjoying a Marlboro, a Coke, a Hershey bar, and listening to No Sugar Tonight in air-conditioned comfort.

Even though I could see the insanity of it all, it was still an exciting adventure we relished. The other revelation that came to me over the mountains of Laos was more of a psychological phenomenon.

One cloudy day we were operating out over Laos against a determined enemy. The opposition had several favored weapons they used in their fight against the deadly Cobra gunships. One was a .51 caliber weapon that manifested itself with long red tracers appearing like red needles. The other was a 37 mm anti-aircraft gun further identified as the same type weapon Jane Fonda posed for pictures on as she was providing aid and comfort to the boys up in Hanoi. That particular weapon manifested itself with large round tracers that looked like yellow balls flying up at you.

The first time I encountered ground fire I was distracted to say the least, and would do such things as scream in the radio, "I'm taking fire! I'm taking fire!" As if that would have done any good.

And then on that fateful cloudy day way out over the kingdom of Laos - it happened. We were operating in a particularly active environment where there were lots of red needles and yellow balls flying in the air. Suddenly I was hit! Hit with a revelation that is. I could hear what sounded like a chorus of angels singing with a 1,000 trumpets blaring.

Now, at that time in Vietnam there were over 500,000 Americans in theater. There was an equal or greater number of opposing forces arrayed against us, the Americans.

Somewhere down below in that green ocean of trees, a member of the opposition with his hand on the trigger looked up in the air at all those aircraft. He looked left, he looked right, he looked high, he looked low, and he picked one aircraft out of the crowed sky and started firing. That aircraft was mine!

As the tracers flew past my canopy closer than I had ever experienced, I was suddenly hit with the revelation that I was special! Someone down there amongst the opposition had picked me out of that crowd up above.

I had never before considered myself to be special. In school I had never been voted the most likely to do anything, I had never been recognized for any great achievements; the school counselor even laughed out loud when I announced to her I was going to the University of Florida.

But on that cloudy day way out over the kingdom of Laos, I suddenly realized I was special. It changed everything. Suddenly all those red needles and yellow balls flying by my canopy no longer distracted me.

For the first time I concentrated fully on doing my job and it was hard. Firing rockets from an unstable platform like a rotary wing aircraft was difficult.

But I concentrated and I concentrated and today I can say without a doubt in my mind - when my tour of duty was over, I was the greatest rocket shooter there had ever been.

In later years I used that same mindset in my business pursuits and it worked there too. One of my businesses, the Naples Marble Company, grew from a small start up in a rental unit to become the largest cultured marble manufacturer in the state of Florida.

It can be said my eyes were opened in the skies way out over the Kingdom of Laos.

There was one other thing I realized about the Vietnam Conflagration during Lam Son 719. It was being waged by one side with a willingness to sacrifice an unlimited number of their people for a cause. Their opponent had an unlimited capacity to accommodate their willingness to kill all their children as a means to an end.

30 - Back Home to Phu Bai

After two months out at Khe Sanh supporting the South Vietnamese Army in Lam Son 719, the South Vietnamese leadership declared victory. With that we packed up and went home to Phu Bai.

At first it was nice to relax from the constant high intensity flying we had conducted over Laos. But things were changing. It was mid-1971 and the Americans were beginning to execute the withdrawal from Vietnam as promised by President Nixon. The mission requirements of the 101st Airborne Division were declining, thus it was becoming highly anticlimactic compared to what we were used to.

Another change happened when our highly respected battery commander, Major Mills, was relieved of command after he beat up the supply sergeant. The unfortunate occurrence resulted from the failure of the assault recipient to properly secure a shipment of weapons returning from our base at Khe Sanh.

Things were not the same without Major Mills, despite his sometimes eclectic and enigmatic behavior. He was an excellent officer and the epitome of what a commander should be, except for one short- coming: the tendency to use physical force as a method of enforcing discipline.

Upon our return to Phu Bai I only had a little over two months remaining on my second tour. With the lack of constant fire missions to keep us busy and a short timer's attitude to boot, I would sometimes drift over the bounds of proper behavior of a dedicated Army officer.

A few days after our return my pilots and I were sitting on hot status. There wasn't much going on so I decided to redecorate the ready room with some art showing our disdain for the seemingly ubiquitous peace symbols that were appearing everywhere.

The inspiration for the artwork came from something I remembered seeing on a mysterious person we met on a CCN mission. It was in the shape of a hand grenade with an inscription reading, "F*** Peace."

I procured some paint and from memory created a real fine reproduction of the grenade and the inscription on the wall of the ready room. It was appreciated by all, with the notable exception of a news correspondent who had stopped by for some follow-up interviews on our adventures in Lam Son 719.

When the reporter saw my artwork he literally went crazy. He was screaming, ranting, and raving as to how anyone could express such sentiments and demanded to know the identity of the perpetrator. He was a small little fellow so I told him I was the artist and inquired as to the reason for his dissatisfaction. Actually I knew the source of his displeasure and couldn't have cared less.

I didn't even mind having to explain my actions to the higher ups after he complained. After the things Jed Duvall and others said about us out at Khe Sanh I was not overly worried about what he thought. I was not running for office.

Another change was occurring with fellow pilots. The old guys were beginning to rotate back home and they were being replaced in several cases by pilots who were older in age, married, and had children. In the past most of the pilots in the battery were young, single, and crazy, with a penchant for excessive risk taking. We began to have new guys coming in and expressing concern for their families in the event of their untimely demise.

We never thought of such things and pitied them in a way. Most of the original guys and I approached our job with a "give 'em hell" mentality, as if there was no tomorrow. Personally, I think that is the better approach in a life or death situation like a war. They also did not get rowdy at the 85th Evac Officers Club as we were sometimes prone to do.

Nothing really exciting happened in my last two months with the 101st. It was spent doing a few routine missions. There were no more big operations in the A Shau Valley or Firebase Ripcord.

The most notable event was when I made the startling discovery I really didn't care for flying. This was especially shocking considering all the effort I had expended to become an Army Aviator. I really thought I loved flying.

This occurred about a week before the end of my tour. As previously stated, a Cobra gunship has space for only a pilot and co-pilot. Consequently, unlike other Army helicopters, the crew chiefs did not fly with their aircraft on missions. So for the benefit of the crew chiefs, efforts were made to allow them to fly in their aircraft whenever possible.

I was walking by the maintenance office and was asked if I would take a crew chief up and fly an aircraft into its PM (periodic maintenance). If an aircraft did not have enough available time before its next scheduled PM for a mission (1.5 hours), it would have to be flown administratively into the PM time slot.

It made no sense to me to fly an aircraft for 35 minutes just to get the flight hours up to the required time for a PM. I suggested to the maintenance officer (Captain Scruggs, my favorite, had already gone home) to just go ahead and do the PM 35 minutes short of the required time, but he insisted it had to have the required time for a PM.

Actually, I didn't mind flying the time for them but I could not resist questioning the logic of the situation. I loved to fly and would take any opportunity to pull pitch. The crew chief was all excited when I told him to hop in and let's go.

We took off and for the first time I did not have any particular place to go. There was no rush, and I did not have to check with the Gia La Artillery Advisory. I decided to head out to Eagle Beach where there was a recreation area. We flew over the beach and the crew chief waved at the guys relaxing by the water. He was having a great time. We then flew down near Firebase Rock Crusher to view a scenic mountain.

Then I began to look at my watch, wondering when the 35 minute joy ride would be over. It was the first time I was bored in a Cobra. Always before, the time flew by and it seemed like we had to turn around for home as soon as we took off. Finally we had flown the obligatory 35 minutes and I landed. After we shut down, the crew chief hopped out and was elated. I just sat there in the seat for a few minutes, contemplating what just happened.

In my previous two years of flying I had never been bored. During the year of flight school there was never a dull moment because we were constantly challenged to learn new things. In a year of flying ARA missions I never tired of piloting the Cobra, but on that 35 minute administrative flight I got deathly bored. It was a shocking revelation that I would prefer to drive on a road and look at the houses, trees, buildings and other cars rather than bore holes in the sky.

31 - The Ending

After two years in Vietnam my Asian adventure was coming to a close. Like all such things I was contemplating the end with both relief and nostalgia, with a dash of melancholy added to the mix. I had seen a lot and amassed a lifetime of experiences both good and bad.

I turned over command of my beloved flight platoon to Captain Phil Bergfield. I wished him and the platoon the best, but it was not to be.

Sadly only a few days after I left the battery, my entire former platoon was killed while flying a night mission near Firebase Rifle. It was shocking news to me because there had been no pilot fatalities during my year with the battery and because I knew the four pilots very well.

They were:

Captain Phil Bergfield - a good officer and dedicated to his job. I will always remember that "Dante's Inferno" night at Khe Sanh when the two of us charged after a North Vietnamese sapper. Phil had a .38 six shooter which was the only weapon between us. I was amazed how he was able to shoot on the run and hit the enemy in the buttocks. We were the only Cobra pilots in battery history to capture a bad guy on the ground. He left a widow who was a nurse assigned to the nearby 85th Evac Hospital.

Lt. Terry Martell - One of my favorites. He was a big talker and some of his claims were a little improbable, such as being a former Boeing 707 pilot. I still enjoyed his company very much. Not one to sit around in idleness he was always doing something. One of his hobbies was photography.

He would take lots of pictures and then go down to the hobby center and develop the prints. He was no Ansel Adams but I still treasure the pictures he gave to me back then. Neither did he suffer from the mediocre food at the consolidated mess facility. He set up his own kitchen in his room, with a hot plate and a wide variety canned foods. The meals he whipped up in his makeshift kitchen were quite good.

The funniest thing I remember about Terry was when he and a Warrant Officer Booker from B Battery attended a conference down in Saigon. Terry was no shrinking violet but he paled when compared to WO Booker's BSing abilities. Terry recounted how when the conference started, the two were sitting next to each other on a bench and they were asked to introduce themselves to the other attendees. WO Booker spoke first and stated, "Booker is the name, killing is the game,

ARA is the way." Terry said at that remark, he slowly slipped down the bench and put as much distance as possible between himself and WO Booker for the rest of the conference.

CW2 Scott Schettig was a young New Yorker full of life who also liked to talk. He once told a story about one of his dating experiences that still makes me chuckle to this day. It seems he was going on his first date with a young lady who lived in one of those classic New York City apartment buildings that featured a few steps leading up to the entrance. He was already a little nervous about meeting the girl's family and could see them watching from the second story windows as he approached. He was so flustered he stumbled on the top step, fell, and rolled down the steps to the sidewalk as the family members watched. He said he calmly picked himself up, dusted off, and proceeded up the steps successfully the second time and went up to meet the family.

1LT Gary Tomlinson was new to the battery when I left so I did not get to know him very well. What I remember about him was he was a fine young man who was quiet and very courteous. It was sad the Lord had to take him at such a young age.

It was such a shame for these fine young men to be taken away so early in their lives. Frequently, it was puzzling why some people died and others lived. Often times I would see people die and wonder, why are they dead and why am I alive? This makes you very thankful to be among the living and prayerful for those taken away before their time.

Finally the day came to pack my belonging and leave. The journey I was about to begin had a curious aspect to it.

There is no doubt in my mind I have a guardian angel watching over me very closely. There have been too many incredible instances in my life to explain it any other way. As I told you earlier, I have even given my angel a name; I call him Gabriel because I figured that would be a good name for an angel.

Apparently he wanted me to get home fast. From the moment the truck picked us up at the battery orderly room, I never stopped until I was sitting in my father's old easy chair, back home in Ocala.

The truck took several of us from our battery to the Division Admin office for out-processing and getting manifested for a flight to Cam Rahn Bay. Upon arrival we were informed that due to unexpected circumstances, there would be space for only two passengers on the C-130. The two names on the manifest were read out and one was mine. The other guys were rescheduled for a flight the following day.

Naturally I cried a few alligator tears for my disappointed compatriots as I hustled out to the soon-to-be-departing aircraft. Those poor guys had to sweat out another night in Phu Bai. An unspoken superstition caused many to fear getting killed during their last week in country.

During the flight to CRB, I was remembering my first tour when I came in country at the same facility. I had had to suffer through several days of watching the departing soldiers swagger around with the smugness of being done with it and on their way home. I was thinking, now it is my turn to loll around the club with my Vietnam suntan and tell the incoming new guys what they were in for.

But it was not to be. Upon arrival at the processing office at CRB, as soon as I signed in and was assigned a bed, I heard my name on the loudspeaker followed by instructions to report to the processing office.

That was quite easy since I was already in the processing office. They informed me there was one remaining seat on a departing PanAm 707 and I was chosen to fill the seat. It was one of those moments of mixed emotions. On the one hand I had relished the thought of swaggering around the balmy CRB environs for a few days and enjoying the moment razzing the newbies. That desire lasted about five seconds when I told the clerk to get me on that plane because I did not have time for a fast train. I happily threw my bag on the olive-green Army bus and headed for the airport.

Just like at the end of my first tour, the same emotions filled the air in the cabin of the departing airplane. Everyone sat quietly as the pilots wasted little time taxiing out to the runway and roaring off. As soon as the plane lifted off there was again that concerted sigh of relief and we all joined in a deafening rebel yell. We could finely stop holding our breath after a year of uncertainty.

Flying back to McChord AFB at Seattle-Tacoma, we again experienced that Twilight Zone phenomenon. Whatever time and date you depart Vietnam you land at McChord AFB at the same time and date.

Upon arrival at McChord I wasted little time in heading over to the Seattle-Tocama Airport and finding a flight leaving immediately for Orlando. I barely had time to call my widowed mother and tell her to fire up my Oldsmobile Delta Royale and head to the airport at Orlando.

She and my younger brother were there to meet me when I landed, and we drove straight home to Ocala. I had just traveled half way around the world non-stop.

And so ended my Vietnam adventure.

Index

Avdeef, 153

B

B Battery, 190, 191, 209, 302
B-52, 178, 217, 258, 259, 265
bamboo vipers, 114, 117
Barry Martens, 277
Bastogne, 187, 207
Bell Helicopter Company, 157
Bennie Hill, 282
Blue Max, 212, 231
Bong Son, 87, 88, 91, 92, 95
Bragg Boulevard, 79
Bushnell, Florida, 9

C

C model gunships, 263
Cactus Motel, 148, 161
Caltex, 72
Cam Ranh Bay, 14, 19, 73, 126, 185
Cambodia, 56, 106, 228, 247
Camp Eagle, 186, 187, 190, 191, 192, 203
Camp Evans, 187
Canada, 12
Canadian Club, 150
Cape Fear River, 79
Capt. Medina, 54, 55
Cary D. Allen, 113, 118
CBS, 62, 248
CCN, 224, 225, 226, 296
central highlands, 20

Central Highlands, 20, 23, 49, 51, 95, 96, 118
CH-53 helicopters, 263
Chu Lai, 47, 58, 77, 78, 79
Clint Eastwood, 183
Cobra gunship, 134, 140, 157, 158, 171, 174, 178, 181, 183, 186, 209, 273, 288, 298
Cold War, 10, 178, 249
Communism, 10

D

Dak Seang, 105, 106, 107, 108
Dak To, 23, 31, 105, 106
Dale Earnhardt, 85
Daleville, 162, 171
Danang, 63, 206
Darvon, 111
Dean Acheson, 250
DEROS, 122
Desmond Dekker, 145
Devils in Baggy Pants, 136
Division Support Command, 31
Duc Pho, 40, 45, 47, 50, 51, 52, 53, 58, 87, 90, 113, 119

E

Enari, 16, 21, 22, 28, 30, 33, 40, 92, 95, 97, 100, 103, 108, 125, 126, 287
Enterprise, 162
ESSO, 72

Quartermaster Corps, 24, 25, 32, 34, 140
Qui Nhon, 21, 25, 46, 51, 63, 64, 65, 69, 70, 71, 76, 79, 80, 82, 87, 97

R

Regular Army Commission, 23, 140
Richard L. Mills, 195
Richard Nixon, 56
Richard Petty, 16, 40, 41, 42, 69
Rick Scruggs, 192, 193, 268
Robert Duvall, 57
Rolling Stones, 107, 290
Ronnie Pepper, 192, 238, 268
Ross G. Carter, 136, 137
ROTC, 11, 23, 24, 134, 141, 205
Roy Rogers, 146, 210

S

Sam Mitchell, 266
San Antonio, 158, 159, 165
San Francisco, 104, 183
sappers, 127, 279, 280
Sarasota, 15, 16
Savannah, 176, 177, 182
Scott Schettig, 13, 303
Seattle-Tacoma, 14, 306
Seguin, Texas, 160
Shell, 72, 73
shocking revelation, 300
Silver Star, 210
Sinclair Refining Company, 71

Skipperville, 108, 162, 163
South China Sea, 49, 119, 187, 207, 225
South Vietnamese Army, 61, 83, 227, 230, 233, 238, 239, 279, 295
Specialist Dula, 283, 284, 285
Standard Instrument Card, 166, 167, 168
Subic Bay, 104, 288

T

Tactical Instrument Cards, 166
Tchepone, 228, 233, 264
Terry Martel, 281
Terry Martell, 13, 302
Tet, 16, 59, 61, 63, 64, 65, 71, 72, 73, 74, 76, 77, 78, 79, 271
Tet Offensive of '68, 61
TH-55, 144, 153, 157, 165, 172
Third Brigade, 16, 40, 45, 48, 49, 50, 54, 58, 59, 76, 87, 89, 90, 91, 92, 97, 98, 100
Three Stooges, 255
Toastmasters, 15, 17
Tony Hoffman, 266, 269
Transportation Corps, 141
Twelve O'clock High, 254
twilight zone, 65, 66, 68, 77
twisted logic, 58

U

Ulysses S. Grant, 17

University of Florida, 11, 23,
134, 141, 204, 205, 293
urban myth, 15
USARV, 186

V

Viet Cong, 14, 85
Vietnam attitude, 29

W

Walter Cronkite, 62, 271, 286
Warrant Officer Candidates, 149
Wayne Burnside, 290
We Gotta Get Out Of This Place,
104
William Calley, 54, 55
Wire Grass, 163
WOC, 149